Teaching with Inquiry

Increasing Student Engagement Across Disciplines

Catherine Snyder
Mary Eads
Sean O'Connell
Richard Lasselle
Sherri Duan
Daniel Mattoon
Patricia Rand

ROWMAN & LITTLEFIELD
Lanham • Boulder • New York • London

Published by Rowman & Littlefield
An imprint of The Rowman & Littlefield Publishing Group, Inc.
4501 Forbes Boulevard, Suite 200, Lanham, Maryland 20706
www.rowman.com

86-90 Paul Street, London EC2A 4NE, United Kingdom

Copyright © 2023 by Catherine Snyder

All rights reserved. No part of this book may be reproduced in any form or by any electronic or mechanical means, including information storage and retrieval systems, without written permission from the publisher, except by a reviewer who may quote passages in a review.

British Library Cataloguing in Publication Information Available

Library of Congress Cataloging-in-Publication Data

Names: Snyder, Catherine Jorgensen, author.
Title: Teaching with inquiry : increasing student engagement across disciplines / Catherine Snyder, Mary Eads, Sean O'Connell, Richard Lasselle, Sherri Duan, Daniel Mattoon, Patricia Rand.
Description: Lanham, Maryland : Rowman & Littlefield, [2023] | Includes bibliographical references. | Summary: "This book is written for teachers who want to make their classrooms an interactive and vibrant place to learn"— Provided by publisher.
Identifiers: LCCN 2023007325 (print) | LCCN 2023007326 (ebook) | ISBN 9781475871715 (cloth) | ISBN 9781475871722 (paperback) | ISBN 9781475871739 (epub)
Subjects: LCSH: Inquiry-based learning—Education (Secondary) | Active learning. | Interdisciplinary approach in education.
Classification: LCC LB1027.23 .S585 2023 (print) | LCC LB1027.23 (ebook) | DDC 371.3—dc23/eng/20230310
LC record available at https://lccn.loc.gov/2023007325
LC ebook record available at https://lccn.loc.gov/2023007326

PRAISE FOR *TEACHING WITH INQUIRY*

"This methods book addresses one of the most critical issues that has confronted education professionals over the last couple of decades. How do you meet the competing challenges of preparing students for standardized tests while at the same time develop within them a sense of inquiry and excitement about learning? The methodology proposed by Snyder et al. addresses this question head on and at the same time could provide another dramatically positive outcome for education professionals. The shift in pedagogy to an inquiry learning model has the potential to also revitalize teachers and help in their retention as the model 'partners' them with students rather than holding them solely responsible for the educational process."

—**Anthony G. Collins**, president emeritus, Clarkson University

"*Teaching with Inquiry* is a timely resource for teachers interested in increasing student engagement while simultaneously increasing students' retention of key content. The Inquiry Learning Model creates a dynamic atmosphere in the classroom where students learn valuable skills: collaboration, communication, and critical thinking. The Clarkson team of education researchers and teachers provide the field with a unique approach to discovery learning that is applicable across all disciplines and grade levels. I encourage any new or experienced educator to diversify their instructional repertoire by using this innovative model to complement other strategies and increase student ownership of the learning process."

—**Matt Sickles**, superintendent, Cobleskill Richmondville

"I was immediately engaged with the Inquiry Learning Model because it reminded me of a game, like *Clue*, and I was excited to try and figure out what we were learning about. I also enjoyed it because I didn't need to know much about the topic to fully participate and figure out the connection between artifacts. After the lesson, I immediately started trying to figure out how I could write my own lesson for a Chinese class with an Inquiry Learning Model in mind."

—**Asha Pollydore**, Chinese language teacher, grades 9–12

"We had the pleasure of hosting Dr. Snyder for a professional development session on their Inquiry Learning Model (ILM) for teachers using primary sources at the Museum. The workshop was extremely useful and well received by the teachers in the session. The ILM is a very effective and accessible method to integrate the teaching of both content and critical thinking skills. We work with teachers to use primary sources as a platform for inquiry based learning, and the ILM works perfectly with this. By shifting the question generation and framing to the students, the ILM is a more robust method to increase students' understanding, long-term retention, and arguably most importantly their ability to transfer knowledge and critical-thinking skills to other settings. I highly recommend this book as an excellent tool to help educators truly integrate inquiry-based learning into their teaching."

—**Sarah Cahill**, Salem Museum Mistic, museum educator

"After receiving my first taste of the Inquiry Learning Model, I haven't looked back. Across each course that I have had the pleasure to teach, along grade and mod levels, inquiry has played a key role. The Inquiry Learning Model touches on the core of something we as educators seek to do—foster a curious and growth minded approach in our students."

—**Matthew Pinchinat**, social studies teacher and Director of Diversity, Equity, and Inclusion

"It is popular to think that being a successful entrepreneur has a simple formula: (1) hatch a big idea, (2) identify customers, (3) develop a product, (4) find a company to make it for you, cheaply, (5) promote on social media, and (6) let it change the world. If only it were that easy. Reality is that starting a new business is more like solving a complex puzzle with two problems: missing pieces and extra pieces from other puzzles. The real process is about asking questions, connecting dots, and thinking. Conventional education teaches formulas. The 'Inquiry Learning Model' teaches the real puzzle-solving process."

—**James Fay**, chemical engineer, inventor, entrepreneur

Contents

PART I: INTRODUCTION   1

Chapter 1: Using Inquiry as a Tool for Learning   3

Chapter 2: Teaching Students to Question Their Ideas   9

Chapter 3: Leading Students to Discovery with the ILM   15

Chapter 4: ILM for All: Accommodations and Differentiation   33

PART II: LESSONS   45

Chapter 5: Lesson 1: The Disappearing Aral Sea (History/Earth Science)   47

Chapter 6: Lesson 2: Let's Travel to an English-Speaking City (World Languages/TESOL)   59

Chapter 7: Lesson 3: Cyclical Modeling: Developing Wave Phenomena (STEM)   67

Chapter 8: Lesson 4: Constructing Chinese Characters (Chinese/History)   77

Chapter 9: Lesson 5: Exploitation and Immortality: The Story of Henrietta Lacks (ELA/Biology/History)   89

Chapter 10: Lesson 6: China's Maritime Might (Economics/History)   101

References   111

About the Authors   115

PART I

Introduction

Today's secondary teachers face a tremendous and competing challenge: obtain excellent and continually higher results on tests that generally only verify rote knowledge, while simultaneously teaching critical thinking, cooperation, and communication skills. Teachers must attend to higher order thinking skills while, often, local and state exams measure only basic literacy, knowledge, and comprehension. The pressure to *teach to the test*, particularly since many state teacher evaluation systems rely heavily on the results of these assessments, can be overwhelming for teachers and students alike.

Additionally, increased emphasis has been placed on ensuring students are college and/or career ready upon graduation. A strong shift toward consumerism is capturing the attitudes of families and students who question the value of postsecondary educational or vocational training programs. Politicians in the past have suggested creating a value metric and increasing competition between colleges and universities to lower costs. Under a system like this, test and evaluation scores will be used to provide these metrics to families, students, and the government.

So, the question becomes, how do we reconcile these social and economic factors with the need to develop critical thinking and collaborative skills so that high school students can be college or career ready?

It is at this intersection of these competing demands that inquiry offers a solution. *Inquiry teaching allows teachers to simultaneously teach content and skills.* And while this book is not recommending teachers use inquiry exclusively, although some teachers do, it is recommending you consider infusing your teaching with inquiry-based lessons at a frequency with which you and your students are comfortable. This book offers one model for your use, the Inquiry Learning Model (ILM).

This book is presented in two parts. Chapters 1 through 4 comprise the first part. In this part you will find a chapter that defines inquiry, a chapter on how to shift the cognitive load of questioning onto the students, a chapter detailing the particular model of inquiry that section two employs, and a chapter that investigates some of the pitfalls of inquiry and how they can be addressed so that an inquiry lesson can meet the diverse needs of the full gamut of learners. After reading part I, you will be ready to take on the lessons found in part II.

There are six sample lessons found in part II. Each lesson comes with background information and step-by-step instructions for how to implement it. The lessons are designed to be interdisciplinary and may be used in one classroom or in collaboration with colleagues who teach other disciplines.

Lesson 1, The Disappearing Aral Sea (History/Earth Science), looks at the ecological disaster that occurred when the Soviet Union diverted water from the Aral Sea for irrigation. Lesson 2, Let's Travel to an English-Speaking City (World Languages/TESOL), is a lesson on geography and world languages. It is presented as a lesson for teaching English but the concept is easily adaptable to any other language. Lesson 3, Cyclical Modeling: Developing Wave Phenomena (STEM), demonstrates a way that mathematics can be taught using inquiry. The lesson could also be used in a science class. Lesson 4, Constructing Chinese Characters (Chinese), is an investigation into the development of the Chinese writing system. While designed primarily for use in a Chinese language class, it can also be used when studying world history. In Lesson 5, Exploitation and Immortality: The Story of Henrietta Lacks (ELA/Biology), students learn about Henrietta Lacks, whose cancer cells were harvested in the early 1950s without her knowledge. These cells were used to test the polio vaccine and have been used ever since for medical research, saving literally millions of lives. Finally, we close the book with a lesson called How Did China Create the First Maritime Global Trade Network? (Economics/History). In this global-history lesson, students explore the life of Zheng He (Jung Ha). Like most of the content in this book, this lesson is multidisciplinary. It has a strong connection to science.

Each of these lessons requires a significant number of digital resources: images, maps, graphic organizers, and so forth. These resources can be accessed from the authors' website, www.inquirylearningmodel.com.

Chapter 1

Using Inquiry as a Tool for Learning

There are not very many teachers who are against the concept of inquiry, but there are precious few who are able to fully put it into practice. Several myths and misconceptions about inquiry persist in education, which prevent many teachers from ever beginning the journey. One such myth is the myth of inefficiency; another is the misconception that students need to have all of the background before they can engage in an inquiry lesson. But these myths are just that: myths with no truth in them.

It is possible to teach very successfully with inquiry as the primary mode of instruction. It is efficient enough to cover all required material, and it is comprehensive enough to bring about the required learning outcomes without much introduction.

Consider this vignette about a math teacher who exhibits the myth of inefficiency. A student in their class is having difficulty with the homework, which involved calculating the surface area of a cone. The student is in a study hall and asks the study hall teacher for help. The study hall teacher loves inquiry, so they engage the student in a discovery lesson using a piece of cardstock with a sector cut out of it. Through a series of questions using the formula for the area of a circle and a proportion, the formula can be derived.

It might take about 10 minutes, perhaps 20 with a full class. Unfortunately, the student was not expected to understand the formula; they were just expected to apply it to solve problems. For many students, this approach is very unsatisfying. Many students want to understand deeply.

When asked where the formula came from, the student said that the teacher told it to them.

Armed with a deeper understanding of the formula, the student would be better able to tackle the problems that they were assigned. If the study hall teacher wanted to cause a little trouble, they might show this method to the math teacher. The math teacher might react in any number of ways; perhaps the most likely is to say something like, "That's neat; I wish I had time to do stuff like that in class."

That is the myth of inefficiency. If a teacher trusts the process and makes the time, they will find that they can still "cover" the material. In a whole class, it might take 20 minutes, but the improved learning outcome far outweighs the cost in class time. The time can be easily recovered by assigning fewer mundane problems.

Many teachers take shortcuts, claiming that they don't have the time to teach with inquiry. It is far too common for children to be introduced to the concept of pi by having the teacher tell them that pi is 3.14. They say that it takes too long to pass out a bunch of soup cans and some string to let the students figure it out for themselves. Of course, there is not one right way to teach things; most concepts can be taught in a number of ways, but perhaps when it comes to pi, there really is only one right way. And it isn't telling the class that pi is 3.14.

Inquiry is a mindset. In order to develop inquiry-based lessons, teachers need to shift their concept of what it means to teach. Many people choose the profession because they loved school as kids and were quite successful at it. Therefore, when beginning a career, a teacher's concept of teaching is probably patterned after how they were taught. Most new teachers have the notion that teaching is primarily the act of telling students information that they ostensibly will remember at some later time. Good teaching, however, is not standing in front of a room and giving students information; good teaching is giving students an opportunity to learn.

Many teachers—the authors included—have been successful teaching an entire course nearly exclusively with inquiry and "cover" as much material as a traditional approach. The myth of inefficiency is just that, a myth. It may take longer to derive a formula for the area of a cone than to tell it to the students, but, at the end of the derivation, students are much further along than those taught by direct instruction.

In physics class, it is common practice to lecture one day and do a lab the next that confirms the concept taught the day before. This is backward. There is one school of thought that disagrees with this. That is the "Isaac Newton already figured this out, so why should we reinvent the wheel?" philosophy. But there is something to be said for figuring it out, something to be said for purposefully reinventing the wheel. What follows is an alternative to lecturing when teaching about the relationship between force and motion.

Based on the premise that the learning will be deeper and more meaningful if students are engaged in a discovery process, a better approach would be to set up some of the same experiments that Newton did and see if they can come to the same conclusions. This teaches them the same content and it teaches them the processes of science as well.

Therefore, in an inquiry classroom, teachers can begin by setting up some experiments and having the students engage in them. The classroom can be set up in stations: a ramp, carts to pull, an Alka-Seltzer® bottle rocket, a pendulum, a motion sensor. At each activity, the students gather data and answer a few questions that get them to begin looking for a relationship.

The overarching question that each activity is based on is this: What is the relationship between force and motion? Each activity has a few questions that accompany it that get students to begin processing the results of that station. As an example, in the motion sensor activity, the students will move in front of the sensor according to a given script. The computer makes a graph of the motion in real time. Then students answer questions such as, "How does the position-time graph show whether you are moving forward or backward?"; "How does the velocity-time graph show whether you are moving forward or backward?"; and "How do the two graphs show whether you are moving slowly or quickly?"

This station can be done at any time in the sequence because each station stands on its own. In order to understand the relationship between force and motion, students need a firm grasp on how motion looks on a graph. This one station contributes to the ultimate building of the concept. The other stations contribute a different piece of the puzzle. The way to design this station activity is to imagine all of the contributing factors that students will need and to design an activity that will help them to build that part of the overarching concept.

Most likely on the first iteration of an activity, there will be some gaps. That is, there will be some parts of the concept that the students will not have developed from working through the stations. The temptation when this happens is to revert to telling the students the missing information. An inquiry teacher will take a different approach; they will ask themselves, "What other activity can I add that will contain the missing piece?"

In the case of forces and motion, it is highly probable that completing the stations will not lead to them being able to discover the first two laws of motion, namely, Newton's First Law, which states that in the absence of an unbalanced force, there is no change in motion, and Newton's Second Law, which states that force causes acceleration.

Upon looking critically at their level of understanding, a teacher might find that the root of the issue is that their concept of acceleration is too narrow. In order to get to the conclusion, an activity that will broaden their concept of acceleration is needed.

Students will accept that force can sometimes stop an object but they may not, due to their narrow concept of acceleration, accept that this is an example of force causing acceleration. Being an inquiry teacher means that it has to be in your mind to search for activities rather than to develop a lecture to solve a problem. It is not, "What can I tell the students to help them get there?"; it is, "What additional activity can I provide to help them get there?" That is where an acceleration detector fits in.

The acceleration detector is a very simple device. It is an inverted soda bottle filled with water and a cork attached to the inside of the lid. When the detector is not being accelerated, the cork stays in the middle straight up. When it is being accelerated, the cork points in the direction of the acceleration. Interacting with this device can broaden their concept of acceleration.

The questions prompt them to interact with the detector in seven different ways and report the position of the cork, then to state whether this interaction is an example of acceleration. Here is a summary of the results:

- Standing still: The cork stays in the center. This is not acceleration, which is not surprising because it agrees with their original concept.
- Starting to move: The cork points forward but only for a second. Starting to move is acceleration. This is also not a surprise because starting to move is a form of speeding up.
- Walking steady: The cork stays in the center. This is not acceleration, which is also not surprising in that it agrees with their original definition of acceleration.
- Stopping: The cork points backward but once you stop, it goes back to the center. This one is surprising. Since most students define acceleration as "speeding up," the action of the cork contradicts their concept. An open-minded student who is willing to rely on the data will state that the acceleration detector shows that stopping is acceleration. A closed-minded person will simply refer back to the original concept and state that stopping is not acceleration because you are slowing down and acceleration is speeding up.
- Speeding up: The cork points away but only as long as you can keep increasing your speed.
- Slowing down: The cork points toward you while you are slowing down. This is acceleration.
- Turning: The cork points in the direction you turn. Turning is acceleration.

The end result of using this detector is that students redefine acceleration as "any change in motion, either speed or direction." Armed with this, they are better able to conclude that acceleration is caused by force.

If you are going to be an inquiry teacher, you need to make it a part of how you think. When given the task of developing a lesson, it needs to be at the core of your philosophy to think, "What experiences can I provide to help students learn this material?" This is the paradigm shift that is required to really be an inquiry teacher. It takes time but you can start today. This book is designed to help you take the first step. Enjoy the journey!

Chapter 2

Teaching Students to Question Their Ideas

Why is it important students ask questions?

> *"The mind, once stretched by a new idea, never returns to its original dimensions." Ralph Waldo Emerson.*

In many classrooms today, students are often tasked to answer rote questions but rarely given the opportunity to develop their own. This learning environment creates students who memorize simple answers to complex problems; students who respond only to what the teacher is thinking, what the teacher believes they should learn and know. But what about students' natural inquiry?

Metacognition on the part of students, where real thinking and discovery of new ideas is supposed to take place, is rarely given space to develop in classrooms today. We need to better prepare our students to activate their curiosity, to ask questions that challenge assumptions about their thinking, and ignite their own learning.

We need to flip the classroom script. When teachers use inquiry, the cognitive heavy lifting is placed on the students, not the teacher. Students are expected to develop questions that will help them discover meaning and uncover truths rather than wait for teachers to present all that information for them. Students' inquisitive nature drives thinking and learning. They are more apt to remember because they are more involved—they are creators of their own knowledge, which makes them more invested in their own thinking and learning.

So how does a teacher flip this script? While the preparation and execution of an inquiry lesson can seem daunting, this does not mean the teacher relinquishes control of the classroom or the learning process; rather, it means that teachers design lessons differently, ones that ignite curiosity and engagement in content: lessons that inspire collaboration, critical thinking, and problem solving. Inquiry lessons are intentionally designed and structured to capture students' attention and focus their energies on solving real-world dilemmas and unpacking known truths. Teachers still plan and deliver instruction, but with a deliberate focus on critical thinking and inquiry. Giving students opportunities to think differently about what they are learning, and having them seek answers rather than receive them, curates a more active, engaged classroom. In this text, we have provided detailed steps on the use of inquiry and also include here several sample lessons for you to consider as models. These have been field-tested and refined with hundreds of middle and high school students across the Northeast during the past decade.

The Inquiry Learning Model (ILM) is adaptable across the disciplines, and while the outcomes may differ depending on the content, the effectiveness and implementation of the model is consistent. Briefly, this model uses a series of prompts, or "clues," to build students' understanding of a topic. The teacher selects the prompts and puts them in a particular order. While this teaching model is very student centered, it is also very much teacher structured. Once the students receive a prompt, they will develop in their groups a series of questions answerable with a yes or a no.

By insisting that students draft questions answerable with a yes or a no, the heavy cognitive lifting is shifted to the student, and away from the teacher. This simple step, of insisting on yes/no questions, transforms the students' role, investment, and learning. This is true regardless of the ILM content area. (For specific details about how the model is enacted, please see chapter 3.)

In the humanities and social sciences, ILM lessons tend to be more about complex, interdisciplinary ideas that have no right or single answer. In science, mathematics, and technology, ILM lessons tend to be about complex concepts with clear, substantiated, theory-based answers. ILM lessons in world languages may be either: very concrete, as may be the case teaching a grammar rule; or very complex conceptually, when teaching about a historical event or a cultural concept.

What is important to note is that the ILM is adaptable to all disciplines and results in powerful learning in all disciplines. It is up to you, the teacher, to decide how to implement the model in service to your students' learning needs.

WHAT CAN WE LEARN ABOUT INQUIRY FROM SCIENCE PEDAGOGY?

The model and lessons described in this book allow teachers to teach fundamental facts and concepts as well as critical thinking, cooperation, and communication skills through an authentic-inquiry approach. Authentic inquiry involves the structuring of a lesson so that students investigate concepts using resources (maps, graphs, primary-source documents, news articles, artifacts, etc.) to develop a multifaceted perspective that allows them to then draw conclusions and come to new conceptual understandings.

The term "authentic" is used in front of inquiry to emphasize that the work done in this type of lesson is authentic to the task a professional would do. In our case, the analysis of artifacts and documents, in an attempt to learn about and answer a compelling question, is the work of scientists, statisticians, historians, researchers, writers, policy makers, educators, lawyers and others who rely on the interpretation and synthesis of knowledge to successfully do their jobs.

Science teachers have long recognized the power of inquiry, and authentic inquiry, in student learning. Indeed, a well-designed science class is built around laboratory activities where students inquire about different scientific concepts, much in the same way scientists do. There is ample evidence in science education that inquiry methods are not only highly effective, but also engaging and adaptable to diverse student populations. In science classes, inquiry usually takes the form of a lab in which students work through a pre-established model. Once understood, models are a particularly powerful tool in any discipline because they allow students to transfer information to disparate situations, allowing for deeper and greater understandings of content.

Lorraine Grosslight (1991), a science-education researcher, identified a predictable pattern in students' understanding of models. They typically move from understanding the model as a one-to-one representation of the topic under study to, at the high end, recognizing the model as a tool to be used to foster greater understanding. The ILMs presented in this book use inquiry as a tool to generate a deep understanding of a topic that can then be applied to other situations. The ILM also allows teachers to teach both content and skills simultaneously.

An example might be helpful to illustrate this point: one of the lessons in this book focuses on the geopolitical crisis suffered by the Aral Sea region in central Asia. In the 1950s, the Soviet Union made the decision to divert water from two rivers that fed the Aral Sea. In doing so, the Aral Sea was effectively destroyed along with the land surrounding the sea. As the water level dropped, the water became increasingly salty. This resulted in mass fish die off and the closing down of the fishing industry around the sea in Kazakhstan and Uzbekistan.

Also, as the water receded, fertilizer that would drain into the sea from the nearby agricultural areas dried on the seabed, became airborne, and caused an increase in deaths from lung disease and a dramatic increase in birth defects. Finally, as the crisis unfolded, and the Soviet Union fell, Kazakhstan and

Uzbekistan struggled to manage the disaster left behind. In the midst of these crises was also the dilemma of what to do with a weapons-testing facility the Soviets built on what was an island in the former Aral Sea.

Once a secure island location for high-risk research, as the water levels receded, the island became a peninsula and then part of the surrounding land. No precautions were taken by the Russian government to secure the facility in 1991, thus leaving behind an international environmental, human-rights, and geopolitical crisis.

Students with a strong understanding of models as tools of analysis and a comprehensive understanding of the Aral Sea crisis from the ILM lesson will understand how this lesson might apply to other potential crisis areas. They might also recognize the usefulness of the information as a template, so to speak, for understanding the underlying reasons for environmental or geopolitical conflict. Inquiry teaching and learning, and in particular the ILM, allows students to develop an initial fundamental understanding of the topic, while simultaneously developing larger conceptual understandings. A teacher who uses ILM can refer back to those concepts when teaching other related material throughout the school year.

Chapter 3 outlines in detail the steps involved in teaching an ILM, but it is important to point out that the ILM may be used in many different ways; teachers can use an ILM in an abridged way as an introduction or anticipatory set, or in its full version as a complex lesson that might span 80 minutes of instruction. Because the ILM is a memorable learning experience for students, teachers can rely on students making connections across the curriculum.

YES, BUT I NEED TO ALIGN MY TEACHING TO MY DISCIPLINE'S STANDARDS . . .

Good point. As a future or current teacher, you are by now aware of the need to align your lessons to the standards of your discipline and the expectations of your school. In addition to the importance of standards, lessons need clear, measurable objectives. A quick review of the objectives written for the lessons showcased in this text reveals the use of all levels of Bloom's Taxonomy (1993), allowing teachers to teach factual information, comprehension, and application as well as critical thinking, communication, and cooperation skills. While planning an ILM often starts with an idea or an artifact, it is vitally important that the next step should be establishing the scope of the lesson and learning outcomes through the crafting of specific learning objectives.

YES, BUT INQUIRY TAKES TOO MUCH TIME . . .

The authors' experience refutes the claim that time is a barrier. In fact, we have found that the time spent using inquiry, and specifically the ILM, increases students' ability to retain key concepts and terms as well increasing their level of engagement with the material. By having to grapple with topics through critical analysis and questioning, students are able to move the material under study from short- to long-term memory—making it available for their future use.

This method facilitates students' deeper understanding of complex ideas, concepts, or models. When students are taught to ask relevant questions based on precisely scaffolded information, they gain deeper conceptual understandings of complex concepts. Once those concepts are learned, their ability to analyze new material, make generalizations, and apply what they are learning to new contexts is strengthened.

Through the gradual introduction of artifacts, the model encourages students to analyze, ask questions, and apply their knowledge as they develop a working theory to answer the focus question. These theories are then tested and discussed by the class in order to comprehensively understand the event, concept, trend, or idea.

The key is selecting concepts that are worth the time. That is, there are concepts central to your curriculum that students need to know in order to be successful. In history, concepts such as conflict, interdependence, or radicalism are worth spending time on because they recur frequently. In mathematics, concepts such as modeling and pattern recognition are central to a student's ability to problem solve.

When confronted with the study of these concepts once through the ILM, students are much more likely to understand and transfer that conceptual knowledge to another setting. In the end, using inquiry deliberately and selectively actually saves time and increases student interest. The lessons selected for this book all represent "big" concepts in the fields of history, mathematics, and language teaching. They were specifically selected to optimize their usefulness across a broad range of curricula.

YES, BUT INQUIRY ONLY WORKS WITH HIGH-ACHIEVING STUDENTS . . .

Absolutely not. The authors of this book have developed and field-tested the lessons presented with a wide range of students, from students with special education needs to second language learners, general education students to honors students, upper elementary students to graduate students. As the next chapter will explain, one of the strengths of the ILM is its adaptability.

When you develop your own ILM lesson, you will choose the prompts (artifacts used in the lesson) that your students analyze, and you control the level of challenge presented. We have developed a number of differentiation strategies to assist teachers in making the lessons in this text and lessons you develop accessible to diverse learners. Chapter 4 is dedicated to these differentiation strategies. Armed with them, teachers can ensure that a high level of understanding is attainable for any and all learners.

WHAT DOES THE RESEARCH SAY ABOUT INQUIRY TEACHING METHODS?

Researchers have been formally studying inquiry models since the 1960s. Throughout the decades, substantial empirical evidence points to consistently high and statistically significant positive results. A 2012 qualitative study commissioned by the Nellie Mae Education Foundation indicated that compared to traditional teaching methods, student-centered learning practices like inquiry methods increase student engagement, make learning more relevant to students, allow students to go into more depth, and increase long-term retention.

The ILM design situates students in an inquiry-based, collaborative learning environment, leveraging the benefits of this approach to teaching and learning. Students' conceptual understandings are more likely to increase when they are actively engaged in the learning process rather than when they are engaged in more passive teaching techniques.

The research team working on the development and field-testing of the ILM have witnessed extraordinary engagement, understanding, and retention in test classes. This is true across grade levels and with varying ability levels.

Chapter 3

Leading Students to Discovery with the ILM

To plan for and use the ILM, a teacher must understand the background and research behind it. In the 1960s, a science educator at the University of Chicago named Richard Suchman received a federal grant to research the use of inquiry-style teaching in Illinois classrooms (1962).

The result of that multiyear study was the development of a model that, based on observational and assessment evidence, proved to be highly effective in improving students' conceptual understanding of broad science topics. Specifically, Dr. Suchman worked with teachers teaching complex scientific concepts to fourth-grade students.

Over subsequent years, changes were made to the model until it evolved into what is today commonly called the Suchman Inquiry Model in teaching methods books (Gunter et al. 2003). It is important to recognize that this model is research-based and has substantial data behind it in terms of its validity and effectiveness (Alshraideh 2009).

The original model forms the basis for the adaptation known as the Inquiry Learning Model (ILM) presented in this book. The ILM has been modified to address all disciplines and to meet the demands of today's secondary classroom.

Broadly speaking, the ILM asks students to work in small groups to formulate yes/no questions for the teacher to answer, based on a series of prompts. While analyzing these prompts, students try to find the answer to a larger focus question that has been posited at the beginning of class. With each consecutive round of prompts and yes/no questions asked by the student groups, the students begin to piece together an answer to the focus question. The key to a successful lesson of this design is the yes/no question format. Asking students to develop questions that are answerable with only a yes or a no puts the burden of thinking on the student.

After all the prompts are delivered and analyzed, the student groups develop theories to answer the focus question, share those theories, and have a full-class discussion led by the teacher. By specifically shifting the focus to theory building, you as the teacher are beginning to build the schema necessary for that cognitive shift from the teacher to the student regarding the central focus question all groups are attempting to answer. This is repeated at the end of the lesson once all of the prompts have been revealed. A sample schedule of the lesson is included here.

This chapter details the specific steps necessary to not only teach an ILM lesson, but also create one. This method will work very successfully if you first familiarize yourself with the steps involved. Pay close attention to the tips for executing an inquiry lesson. These tips are based on the authors' years of field-testing and observation. After reading about how to implement an inquiry lesson, you will be able to see ways to differentiate and adapt the model to your specific teaching setting.

Once you have used the lessons in this text, you will likely begin to see opportunities for inquiry lessons in your existing curricular materials, in books you read, or in conversations you have with colleagues. The next part of this chapter provides you with detailed directions for assembling your own ILM lesson. The chapter ends with tips, frequently asked questions, and suggestions for modifications to the model.

HOW TO USE THE LESSONS IN THIS TEXT

The Inquiry Learning Model includes seven steps that will be explained in detail below. The lessons in this text provide you with all the information and background you will need to teach using this model. If you are teaching a topic with which you have limited familiarity, we recommend that you do a bit more research and reading on it prior to teaching the lesson. Each lesson ends with references for extending the learning and for further reading.

Over the years, we have been continually surprised by the questions students ask; even now, every time we use this model, we get asked questions for which we do not know the answers. As you can imagine, the lesson is far more effective if you can answer most of your students' questions with a confident yes or no. Be prepared, however, to be stumped by students' questions and theories. The inquiry and discovery processes encourage divergent thinking, which manifests itself in interesting and often surprising results.

1. select the problem and conduct research
2. introduce process and present problem
3. gather data
4. develop a theory and verify
5. state the rules and explain the theory
6. analyze the process
7. evaluate

Step 1: Investigate and Prepare (Select the Problem and Conduct Research)

This work has been done for you for the five lessons included in this text. Each lesson chapter includes background information for the teacher, a list of references for further reading, and a focus question. Before you teach one of the lessons presented here, you need to organize the resources.

Each prompt is carefully chosen and ordered to allow students to think deeply about a specific inquiry. Keep the prompts concealed until you are ready to present them during the lesson. Part of this process is to engage the natural inquisitiveness of learners; presenting the prompts as a series of clues fosters that inquisitiveness.

Number each set of prompts, if possible, so the lesson unfolds in an orderly fashion. We recommend that you provide only one prompt at a time to each group during the questioning rounds. This encourages students to work together instead of subdividing the analysis of multiple prompts within the group.

In addition to providing only one prompt at a time, we recommend that each group be given only one prompt to share within the group(s). Research confirms that the simple act of providing one prompt to a group of students increased the likelihood that they would work together. Whether the prompt is a map, photograph, piece of rubber, or bag of salt, analyzing only one item encourages interaction and collaboration. The one exception to this might be a lengthy text.

For example, the Aral Sea lesson included in this text ends with two full-page articles. We recommended that you either give each student a copy of the article to read or read the articles aloud to the class. Chapter 4 offers further suggestions for differentiating prompts in mixed-ability classrooms.

After preparing and arranging materials for the class, the next task is forming the groups. As is the case with any group exercise, how you arrange your students into groups depends on your secondary goals. Are you trying to provide opportunities for particular students to learn social and collaborative skills? Are you trying to foster more or less competition among your students? Are you trying to create groups of students that will work well together or support each other? Prearrange your groups based on your learning goals, knowledge of your students, and classroom dynamics. Groups of three are highly recommended when you first start using inquiry.

Collaboration and good listening skills are required, so working with only two other classmates allows students to practice and hone these skills with minimal distraction. If your students have experience sharing resources and ideas, feel free to arrange your groups with four or even five students. Another factor to consider when forming groups is the overall number of groups.

If, for example, you create seven groups of three students each (21 students total), you will be giving your students seven opportunities to ask questions in each round of inquiry. If you have a very large class—40–50 students, for example—you might consider making the groups slightly larger. For example, you might want to put the students into groups of four, resulting in 10–12 groups total.

We have successfully taught with this methodology in classrooms ranging from early high school to graduate school with class sizes from as small as 9 to as large as 55. Keep in mind that the more groups you have, the more questions will be posed by students per round.

The more questions they ask, the further along students move in their thinking with each consecutive round. In the event that you have a very small class, we recommend creating groups of two or three students. You could also allow each group to ask two questions per round so that students have enough information to develop ideas and theories.

Step 2: Introduce Focus Question (Introduce Process and Present Problem)

Once you have organized the resources for the lesson and created your student groups, the next step is to introduce the focus question. The first time you teach an ILM lesson you will need to devote about 10 minutes of class time to introducing the lesson and explaining the rules to students. Teachers use a variety of comparisons to help students to quickly understand the learning process.

At the secondary level, you might refer to this type of lesson as a "Let's solve a mystery" game or a "Clue" game. With more advanced or college students, you might explain that it mirrors the work of professional historians. An advanced placement class, for example, might be motivated by the similarity of the work to that of historians—like finding a long-forgotten box of artifacts in an attic and trying to make sense of them. Other students might be more motivated by the idea of a game. You will want to introduce the lesson differently depending on the age and level of students.

However you decide to introduce the lesson to your students, it is imperative to review the guidelines carefully. A set of guidelines is provided here. We suggest that each group receive a copy of the guidelines and sign it as a commitment to try to follow them. Have copies of the guidelines laminated and placed on desks before the lesson starts so the guidelines are accessible during the entire lesson.

You will only have to spend time explaining the guidelines once. In subsequent uses of the model, you need only refer back to the "Clue" game or other descriptor you use for the methodology with your students.

Once you have reviewed the classroom guidelines, invite students to ask any questions they might have about the procedures for the lesson. The most important point students must understand is that their questions be crafted in such a way that they are answerable by you with a yes or a no (guideline #4). Asking students to develop questions that are answerable only with a yes or a no puts the burden of thinking on the student. At this point, have students sign the contract and select roles. To help students organize information, you may want to assign specific roles to each member of the group.

We recommend that each group have two note takers, a theory writer, and a timekeeper. This organization and role responsibility ensures all students feel that they are now part of that particular team/group, and will work accordingly.

After you are certain the students understand the guidelines, you may show them the focus question. You might want the focus question to be hidden behind a sheet of paper or revealed on a projector screen only when you are ready to begin. This adds a bit of excitement to the lesson because students wonder what is so important about the focus question.

Conversely, you might want to put the focus question on the board so that students see it as they enter the room. As you can see from the table of sample questions, the focus questions are enigmatic, provocative, and open ended. In our experience, the question that most intrigues adolescent and young adult learners is, "So what? Why should I care?" This question seems to appeal to their predisposition to think contrarily toward adults and adult ideas. So, while it sounds almost rude, it is a great focus question for grabbing students' attention right away. Using the example included in chapter 4, invite the groups' note takers to write the focus question at the top of the page.

Step 3: Start Questioning Rounds (Gather Data)

Now you are ready for your students to start working with the prompts. This step is the central piece to the Inquiry Learning Model. During this step you will distribute the prompts, one at a time, to your students. After the first prompt is distributed (one prompt per group), allow students a specific amount of time to analyze the prompt. We suggest 5–8 minutes, depending on the nature of the prompt, the age of your students, their level of experience with analysis and collaboration, the complexity of the prompt, and the length of your class.

If the prompt is a lengthy reading, you may consider increasing the amount of time allotted or reading the prompt aloud to the class as students follow along. Remember that students may become frustrated and confused by the prompts. Spending too much time on one prompt can lead students to disengage if they can find little or no meaning in the prompt. Moving to the questioning round will allow students who are beginning to disengage to see how other groups have advanced their thinking using the prompt. More often than not, this allows students to reengage.

As the students are analyzing the prompt, circulate and listen carefully to their conversations. Students at this stage will try to ask questions to get additional information from you. Respond only with a firm, "That is a great question. Consider asking that when it is your group's turn." It is important to pay attention to the conversations students are having and the questions they are formulating. You might find that you want to arrange the order in which student groups ask their questions to build the class's knowledge of the topic.

If, for example, you observe that one group's analysis is more advanced than others', you may want to call on that group last. By doing so, you give the other groups the opportunity to draw conclusions independently.

The initial lesson prompts in this book are purposefully designed to immediately capture students' attention. The Aral Sea lesson, for example, uses a photograph of fishing boats that appear to be stranded in the middle of a desert. Providing unusual prompts for the first round fosters divergent thinking among the students, which stimulates a broad range of fascinating questions. This is a wonderful chance for students to stretch their imaginations.

Once the analysis time has expired, bring students' attention back to you. At this point you should have an idea of the questions the groups are going to ask and the rough order you will use to call on the groups. Remind students that each group is allowed to ask one question answerable by you with a yes or a no, and that each question will be asked and answered only once. It is important that you enforce the latter guideline, as it is vital to classroom management.

The effectiveness of this lesson lies in the educator's ability to foster competition and cooperation simultaneously. You want students to be enthusiastic and challenged but not so much that it disrupts the lesson. You will notice students correcting each other if they cannot hear the questions being asked. This provides them with the opportunity to self-correct and frees you from the duty of shushing them. Proceed with the questioning round, answering each group's question to the best of your knowledge.

As mentioned earlier, it is imperative that students ask questions in a way that you may answer with a yes or a no. This format is at the heart of the model's success. This seemingly simple shift in classroom responsibility moves the cognitive heavy lifting to the student.

For example, for the Aral Sea photograph of marooned fishing boats, students might ask, "Are the fishing boats marooned because of an ecological disaster?" Because this question is answerable with a yes or no, the students developed a theory to help explain the photograph. Without the yes/

no question format, students might ask, "What happened to the boats?" This question requires no theory development on the part of the students.

Occasionally a group is unable to offer a question. This happens for a variety of reasons. For example, other groups may have asked the questions they were planning to use, or the group may be genuinely stumped by a prompt. You can solve this dilemma in a number of ways: You can give the students 1–2 more minutes to analyze the prompt; you can give the group a free pass for that round, making it okay to *not* have a question; or you can circle back to the group after all the other groups have asked their questions. Often the group that did not have a question earlier is able to ask a question after hearing the other groups' thinking.

You can have some fun with your students during the questioning rounds. We have found that while answering students' questions, it is often not enough to simply say yes or no. That is not to say we elaborate on our answers, but rather *act* on them. If a group asks an especially pivotal question, you might over dramatize your yes or no. Or, if a group asks a question that is just slightly off the mark, perhaps even because of a syntactical element, you might answer yes or no with a flourish of hand gestures implying that they are very close.

Students respond to this play acting quite positively, and either believe or pretend to believe that they are getting more information out of you than you are intending to give them. They begin to watch your reaction very carefully, further fostering an environment of guided inquiry.

Step 4: Unveil Working Theories (Develop a Theory and Verify)

Once the first questioning round is complete, proceed with subsequent questioning rounds in a similar fashion. Leave the prompts with the groups so that the resources accumulate during the lesson. Students often refer back to previous prompts to help them piece together the information gathered during the lesson. At some point, roughly at the midway point, you will want to pause the inquiry process to gauge student thinking. Included here is a sample lesson broken down into "rounds" with anticipated time allocated for each:

Activity	Time allotted	Total time used
Introduction and directions	10 minutes	10 minutes
Round 1	8 minutes	18 minutes
Round 2	8 minutes	26 minutes
Round 3	8 minutes	34 minutes

Round 4	8 minutes	42 minutes
Initial theory	10 minutes	52 minutes
Round 5	5 minutes	57 minutes
Round 6	5 minutes	62 minutes
Round 7	5 minutes	67 minutes
Theories shared and discussed	15 minutes	82 minutes

When you feel the students have enough information to speculate on a one-sentence answer or theory statement to the focus question, ask them to do so. Five minutes is usually enough time for groups to form a theory. As groups are developing their sentences, circulate and lend assistance as needed. You will also want to steer students away from the tendency toward silly hypotheses, such as, "Aliens came down and built the pyramids."

Encourage students to rely heavily on the prompts in front of them and the notes they have taken. If a group is tending toward a silly statement, it is often because they are not processing the information presented thus far. It should be a signal to you to reflect on the particular skills of the learners in that group.

As groups complete their statements, invite the theory writers to write each group's statement on the board along with the first names of the students in the group. Once all the statements are on the board, invite a member of each group to read the statement. Then provide some feedback on the statement. This might take the form of, "Wow, your group is really on track. Everyone, I would pay attention to this statement. You might even want to write it on your note sheet." This is an obvious directive to the students that their thinking is at least right, if not complete.

With other statements you might find yourself underlining particular phrases that are relevant. Even if a group's statement is off track, try to say something positive about it. After all, it represents the students' best thinking on the inquiry so far. A comment like, "Oh, I can see why you might think this, because of XYZ prompt, yes, but I think you should go back and look at that document again, perhaps with ABC prompt right next to it."

In this way you are not completely deflating the group's efforts but also acknowledging that they are not quite on track. This process typically takes about 10 minutes, depending on class size, but it is time well spent as students get to hear what other groups are thinking and add other students' theories to their own.

Once you have moved through all of the statements on the board, resume with the remaining prompts. Remember, the educational goal of an ILM is to allow all students to advance their thinking, and by default, their learning.

Although the lesson is conducted in a competitive format, group versus group, it is important for the teacher to remember that the goal is to allow all students to experience teetering on the edge of awareness. Although one group may get there first, in the end all of the students develop a comprehensive understanding of the topic.

Step 5: Investigate Remaining Prompts (State the Rules and Explain the Theory)

The remaining prompts in an ILM lesson typically tie the topic together and fill in gaps that might exist in students' knowledge. As you move through the last couple of prompts, it is not uncommon to hear lots of excited comments like, "I told you!" and "Remember, I said that!" in groups. Once all the data is in front of the students, it is time to move to the next step.

Implementation tip: Pausing in the process in the middle of the data gathering stage is vital to correcting misinformation and honing student thinking in the right direction.

Step 6: Revise Theories and Discuss (Analyze the Process)

In this step you will invite each group to revisit its theory and modify it based on the new information. This process will take about 15 minutes, depending on students' skill level. Once all the groups are ready, invite each theory writer to stand and read their group's theory to the class. Remember, at this point, your goal is to have the students address the focus question with their theories. It is important not to anoint one group as having the best or most comprehensive answer.

Remember, the point of this model is to encourage students to exercise critical-thinking and collaborative skills. The fastest way to discourage students from trying to think critically and collaborate is to tell them they did not get the *right* answer. It is very important that the educator collect the theory statements written by each group at the end of the lesson. This is a record of the progression of student thinking.

Collecting the statements affirms the work of all the groups, even if one group appears to have a more complete answer before the other groups. Reviewing why specific facts were used to support the theory can be a point for discussion, even if the group drew an inaccurate conclusion. You may also want to make written comments on the submission and share the comments with the groups later.

After each group has presented its revised theory, open the floor for a full-class discussion. Depending on time, this might take place the next day.

In our experience, students really enjoy this part of the lesson because they get the satisfaction of asking questions freely, often in rapid-fire format. You also get to fill in the missing pieces and correct misconceptions that might have surfaced. Depending on the lesson, this might be a short discussion or a discussion that takes an entire class. You will be surprised at the high level of engagement your students have at this stage of the lesson.

Step 7: Evaluate and Reflect

The last step has to do with encouraging the students to be metacognitive about their learning. That is, you want to foster in them the habit of reflection about their own learning process by asking them to evaluate and reflect on their work. You are asking them to reflect on how well they performed as group members, assess the level of effort they put into the lesson, and evaluate their own learning as a result of the lesson.

Using the Evaluation and Reflection worksheet available on the authors' website (see preface), ask students to answer the questions honestly and to write a short reflection about what they might do differently if the class does a similar activity in the future. Save these documents and hand them to the students, with the suggestions they made to themselves highlighted, just before you embark on another ILM lesson. Be careful not to grade these reflections; otherwise, students will be more reserved and prescriptive in what they write.

You can end the lesson with a full-class discussion, an individual homework assignment, or any number of formal or informal assessments. The lessons in this text offer ideas for assessments tailored to each of the topics.

TIPS FOR EXECUTING AN INQUIRY LEARNING MODEL LESSON

While field-testing the lessons in this book, we encountered challenges that had to be addressed during instruction. Below is an account of those challenges, followed by suggestions for managing them. Lessons were field-tested in classes with students ranging from secondary to graduate level.

A Student-Centered Model

Because this is a student-centered model, sufficient classroom management needs to be in place in order for students to act respectfully, share resources, and listen when peers ask questions. If the students have not previously been given the types of responsibility they will need, it might be advisable to take small steps toward using an ILM lesson.

For example, before teaching an entire lesson in this manner, give the students one artifact as a class opener or as a group activity. In this way, students gain practice sharing resources, asking questions, and listening to each. This will prepare them for a full lesson using this model. In many ways, the ILM follows the principles of a well-taught cooperative learning lesson. For information on how to teach using cooperative learning, see Spencer and Miguel Kagan's 2009 book on the topic, *Kagan Cooperative Learning*.

A Student Who Knows the Answer

When presenting this model to teachers at workshops, the most common question asked is, "What do you do if a student knows the answer at the beginning?" That is a very important question to consider. Here are some strategies for how we have handled this situation in the past. First, you will most likely know who that student might be. If you do, have a conversation with the student about the importance of letting their classmates figure out the answer on their own. If this strategy is unlikely to work with this student, you can ask them to assist with timing the rounds and passing out prompts.

While this does happen occasionally in the execution of ILM lessons, it does not happen often. More often, a student thinks they know what the lesson is about but after some questioning realizes that they either are off the mark or have an incomplete understanding of the topic.

A Student Figures Out the Answer Early

As is the case with the student who thinks they know the answer, it is also possible that the class will think they have figured out the answer to the question sooner than you expected. This happens rarely because of the complexity of the lessons. You will have to encourage the students to dig much more deeply into the prompts and consider the focus question more broadly.

If, however, you sense that your students are homing in on the discovery sooner than anticipated, you can make changes to the lesson as you are teaching it. For instance, you can distribute a couple of prompts at a time. This moves the lesson along faster but still gives the students the sense of discovery that makes the methodology so powerful.

Several Sections of the Same Class

The power of discovery teaching is that "aha" moment when students come to a realization on their own. It is a great moment for the students and the teacher. The challenge for the secondary teacher, however, is the school schedule. If, for example, you teach a world history class before lunch and another one after lunch, how do you keep your students from talking about the lesson at lunch? This dilemma, of course, is not unique to this particular teaching model and is difficult to address. We have had the most success by simply not saying anything to students. Often it does not occur to them to share class activities with each other.

If you think students in one section will talk to students in another section, ask the first class not to share anything with their peers. After all, they had some fun with this lesson and would probably want the same for their classmates in the afternoon.

Whether or not students comply will depend on their maturity and your relationship with them. In the event that a student enters the room knowing the basic answer to the focus question, it does not preclude them from participating in the discovery process. The student may know what happened, but they still need to understand *how* and *why* it happened.

Addressing Misconceptions

Another common concern raised by teachers about this model is the chance that it might create, rather than clarify, misconceptions. This does not seem to happen; in fact, the opposite seems to be true. Misconceptions tend to be preexisting. An ILM lesson tends to bring to the surface these misconceptions, providing the opportunity to discuss them. In a more traditional type of lesson, these misconceptions may be concealed and not reveal themselves until a culminating assessment. Historical misconceptions are very common in adolescents and take many forms. A recurring theme in the lessons in this book is complexity.

It is very common for an adolescent to see history or science as linear and to enter the classroom with a notion that a single factor caused a particular event. These lessons bring these ideas out and systematically debunk these ideas. In this way students appreciate the complexity of issues and are able to understand the nuances better.

A second common issue with adolescents is a narrowness of perspective. Adolescents and students in general tend to have difficulty seeing the world from a perspective other than their own. An important part of the learning and maturing process is a broadening perspective. An ILM lesson builds understanding and respect for others in this way.

The Students Are Getting Frustrated

Frustration is a genuine emotion students feel when pushed beyond their skill level. It is a real issue that must be attended to when instructing with this model. While you want your students to be engaged, intrigued, and challenged, you do not want them to become so frustrated that they disengage. This can be managed by your careful monitoring throughout the lesson. Circulating among groups during the questioning rounds will give you clear insight into your students' state of mind.

You should see students talking, pondering, and puzzling over the prompts provided to them. This might take the form of animated conversation or quiet contemplation. If, however, you see a student disengaged—leaning back in their chair with arms folded, for example—that is a sure sign that the student has reached a frustration point and is no longer willing to participate.

The key to not letting frustration take control of the learning process is early detection. If you see a student, or a group, in this situation, it helps to redirect their thinking. Perhaps ask the student or group where their thinking is on the topic, point them toward a salient detail, or indicate that a question they have brainstormed is particularly good. When you provide some assistance, students usually jump back on board and become interested in the topic once again.

Calling on the group first, or last, in the next round and calling the class's attention to their question also increases their sense of value and commitment to the lesson. As is the case with all types of teaching, the goal is to keep the student in that liminal space between boredom and frustration (such as boredom–engagement–frustration).

MODIFICATIONS TO THE INQUIRY LEARNING MODEL

One of the strengths of this model is its flexibility. The lessons presented in this text were designed for a 75-minute class; however, they can easily be modified for shorter or longer classes. The prompts in the model may also be used as an anticipatory set or class opener, or as a brief formative assessment.

Teaching an Inquiry Learning Model Lesson over Two Days

If your classes are 35–45 minutes long, you have a few options for modification. First, you could give your students multiple prompts in each round. The lesson prompts in this book are scaffolded so that they gradually build students' knowledge and help them answer the focus question. But often two or even three prompts can be presented at the same time with no loss of comprehension. This allows you to cut the overall class time down considerably.

Another option in shorter classes is to teach the lesson over two days. A natural break occurs in the lesson at the point where students unveil their working theories. This typically happens at the midway point in the series of prompts. You could even embed a homework assignment into the lesson that allows students to conduct some independent research on the topic before resuming with the lesson the next day.

Using This Model as a Class Opener

The strategy used by this model is very compelling as an opening activity for a class. A prompt could be projected on a screen or available on student tablets for them to review upon entering the room. Class could begin with a 20 questions game that engages students in the content to be learned. This strategy increases student interest and ownership in the learning about to take place.

Introducing One Prompt per Day

You could also use this strategy to teach an entire ILM lesson across several days by introducing one piece of the mystery every day. The prompt that opens the class could highlight the topic that will be taught in some detail that day. By using inquiry in this way, it becomes an organizing feature across a series of lessons.

HOW TO DESIGN YOUR OWN INQUIRY LEARNING MODEL LESSON

One of the key elements of a successful Inquiry Learning Model lesson is the teacher's deep content knowledge. Because students can ask any question they want during the lesson, the more you know about the topic the better the lesson will flow. This requirement should not deter you from trying an ILM lesson, however. After all, think about how much your students know about any particular topic.

For example, prior to teaching them about the French Revolution, did your students already know who Robespierre was? Probably not. So, while you need to know your topic well, balance that need with the recognition that you already approach the lesson with far deeper content knowledge and understanding than your students.

Inquiry lessons can be placed at the beginning, in the middle, or at the end of a unit of study. For example, you can use it to introduce a topic that will be explored over the course of a unit, semester, or year, or you can use it as a test for understanding as you wrap up a set of lessons at the end of a unit. It can also be used in the midst of instruction before students fully understand the topic under study.

A good example of this is a lesson using *The Crucible* by Arthur Miller. Prior to students fully understanding all the factors contributing to the behavior of the characters, an ILM lesson could be organized around the theories that exist today that attempt to explain the Salem Witch Trials. The same midstream concept could be used with other topics in history that have interesting turning points.

Once you have selected a topic for your ILM lesson and determined its placement in your curriculum, you need to gather prompts and develop a focus question. Developing the focus question can be challenging. You want to develop a question that is sufficiently vague so as not to point to an answer for the students, but you also want a question that is intriguing and that will lead students down the intellectual path you have created for them. Consider the commonly used Inquiry Learning Model questions provided earlier in this chapter or develop a new one based on your unique lesson.

As you are considering the focus question, you need to also be gathering the prompts for the lesson. Often, interesting prompt ideas are found in books written specifically on the topic of the lesson. For example, Edwin Black's (2012) book *IBM and the Holocaust* is a treasure trove of photographs, maps, and diagrams related to the Hollerith machine used by the Nazis during World War II. This one book provides several choices for prompts. As a teacher, you already read in order to increase your own content knowledge. Once you have used inquiry in your classroom, you will begin to see ILM lessons in the books you read.

Start paying attention to the maps, diagrams, historical photographs, and other resources provided by those books. You will also want to consider trying to collect a variety of prompts: maps, primary source documents, news articles, photographs, artwork, charts and diagrams, and objects. The greater the variety of prompts, the higher the students' interest and chances for success. Some students will respond well to text-based prompts, while others will be able to decipher details from a photograph or a series of satellite images.

After gathering a set of prompts, the next task is deciding the proper order of delivery. Generally, you want to start with a very compelling but obscure prompt to grab the students' interest. Subsequent prompts should build student knowledge of the topic, gradually moving from general to more specific. After you have taught a lesson you designed, you will find you might rearrange the order of the prompts, or add or subtract prompts based on students' interactions with them.

You might also change the prompts based on particular student populations. If, for example, all of your students are studying Spanish, you might want to include a document that makes use of this developing skill. Consider the particular skills your students might have or are learning in other classes when selecting prompts.

The best advice we can give you regarding developing your own ILM lesson is to try the method a few times. The first time students participate in an inquiry lesson, they might be challenged by the format and what you are asking of them. After they have worked through this model a couple of times, their questioning and analytical skills grow tremendously.

You might also need to work through a lesson a couple of times to get the order of the prompts correct or to learn the types of questions your students will ask. You may consider working with a colleague so that the lesson is tested in several classes simultaneously, thus providing more opportunity to adjust the lesson for the following year.

The Inquiry Learning Model is a dynamic and fun methodology that will enliven your teaching and your students' learning. We invite you to start your inquiry teaching with the lessons in this text. Once you are comfortable with the model, build inquiry lessons that align specifically with your curriculum and your students' skills and abilities.

Chapter 4

ILM for All

Accommodations and Differentiation

A CASE FOR STUDENT-CENTERED CLASSROOMS

If you were thinking about visiting a middle or high school classroom for a day, you would have your choice, naturally, of literally thousands of schools across the United States. On your visit, you might peer into a "typical" classroom and see students who are seated in rows arranged in some form of symmetrical fashion, probably five to six per row and somewhere near 30 or so students in those desks total. For example, it's a clear, crisp fall day, and the teacher at the front of the classroom is beginning the day's lesson on a nameless topic for the following 45 minutes, with 30 or so students arranged as above watching and listening.

The students in the class have their notebooks/laptops out and are half-heartedly attempting to write every single word that comes out of the teacher's mouth. Occasionally, when the teacher writes something down, some students place a star or asterisk in the margin of their notebook. This pattern is repeated several times throughout the day, across several subjects, by hundreds of students. The teacher would dictate notes or ideas, students would write them down in a notebook or type into a laptop, and "learning" new topics or concepts on a specific subject was happening.

Or was it? Certainly, it was in the correct environment for learning. Students are seated at a desk, in a school, with a teacher leading the classroom and the instruction. Students had all of the tools of education that were needed at their disposal (computer, paper, pen, etc.). So, were they in fact "learning" new material? Interestingly, if one were to survey teachers in this school building, the concept or action of the verb "teaching" would be used countless times to express the learning taking place. Except, the "learning" didn't really feel like learning to many of the students on this particular day or on countless other days. Students often wondered why there wasn't more discussion or debate with peers about generalized and specific concepts.

Rarely, in some classrooms, there would also be groups of students who would be working on a project or simulated question in a collaborative manner, and it was in those moments when most students would remember specifics about the topics, ideas, themes, or conclusions from their lessons. (Who has not constructed a reproduction of the Shakespearean Globe Theater, or the parts of a plant cell using manipulative reproductions using clay, or launched a rocket to determine the trajectory?) So, how could there be this dichotomy between these two experiences?

In some classrooms, immersion into the learning, or a continuous model of student-centered learning, isn't necessarily the norm. This is, unfortunately, happening too often in schools across America. Additionally, connections to materials previously used often are not evident in some classrooms, as well. Students often comment that concepts are "taught" and not reviewed again until the exam, or even the final exam. There clearly needs to be more student-centered, student-led initiatives of learning in classrooms today.

Moving from the realm of high school to college and beyond and thinking in earnest about students' learning about how students learn, are important concepts for teachers to consider in planning effective instruction. Why are there sometimes so many different variations to the theme of who learns inside a given classroom? Every classroom includes a high degree of variability. For example, there is variability in the discipline taught, the students and their skills, the age range of the students, the context for learning, and the teacher's background, training, and experience. All of these variables, and more, create an environment that presents challenges to both the teacher and the student.

How exactly do students learn? Why does it seem that when students work in collaborative groups, learning seems to increase? Can the use of inquiry in the classroom improve student learning outcomes? Most important, how can teachers include all students in the learning process, especially those who are disadvantaged learners in some way? If the teacher were to use inquiry, can those students who struggle with concepts and skills garner much from a form of instruction that relies on collaboration and consultation with other students? We think the answer is yes to these questions.

The idea that students should take an active role in their learning is nothing new. A quick review of the research shows us that many educational theorists wrote about the value of student-centered learning in classrooms as a means of boosting engagement, thinking, and, ultimately, learning. Johnson and Johnson (1999) wrote extensively about the use of cooperative learning in classrooms as a way to achieve high levels of engagement and learning.

Cooperative learning is not the only example of early attempts that recognized the value of student centered learning. This idea of teacher structured/student centered learning is something that in reality has been written about in education circles for quite some time—perhaps even early human history.

Dr. Richard Mobbs (2008), from the University of Leicester writes that "From various research sources we know that we remember from. . . . : the Lecture (5%); Reading (10%); Audio Visual (20%); Demonstration (30%); Discussion group (50%); Practice by doing (75%) and Teaching others (90%)." He was stating these ideas inside an overall general discussion on the idea of the use of podcasting in today's teaching and learning. So, even with the inclusion of more and more technology into the classroom, there still exists a need for cooperative, collaborative, and consultative group work processes to achieve a high level of student engagement and learning.

Consider the following axiom from the Chinese philosopher, Confucius: "Tell me, and I will forget. Show me, and I may remember. Involve me, and I will understand." So, from the thoughts of Confucius through today, it has been recognized that involving students in their learning is critical if we want engaged, thoughtful students working with complex ideas and concepts. These concepts are useful in furthering student learning and understanding of the content material we are teaching them.

The idea of teacher-structured, student-centered learning is one that has intrigued us for many years. How can we improve our ability to involve students in their learning while maintaining our ideas of active student-centered learning? What types of activities can assist students in achieving this concept? How can I develop an interesting and engaging set of lessons to improve student achievement?

The Inquiry Learning Model

The idea of teacher-structured, student-centered lessons is the heart of our attempt to develop what we think works best in the content area classroom: inquiry learning. Taking this construct, we have developed a model for using inquiry in the classroom to engage and inspire students to learn from one another in an interactive, novel way. We provide for the reader in this text several examples of lessons that we have developed in the humanities, mathematics, and science disciplines.

These inquiry-based lessons are at the heart of what we believe lead teachers to true student learning and achievement in their classrooms. The ILM can be adapted to any subject matter or discipline that you are teaching. It is flexible enough—as you will see once you review the samples included here in the text—and is easily incorporated into your lessons after you become familiar with the steps of the model.

Using the Inquiry Learning Model in Mixed-Ability Classrooms

One question we might want to ask at this point in our discussion is this: How can we assist all of our students to become proficient learners in our classrooms who may struggle with content? Even using ILM, might there be some students who will still struggle because of particular learning abilities? In essence, while using an ILM lesson, how can we improve the learning of students in our classrooms who may be disadvantaged or underserved in some way (learning disabled, second language acquisition, etc.) or see our students for who they are, as individual learners with a set of unique abilities and perhaps some challenges or barriers to learning?

If we think back to our discussion of "learning" in the traditional classroom, we have posited in this text that using more student activity and interaction increases the amount of student learning and student achievement. Our answer to this was the development of the ILM and ILM lessons. However, more than ever, our classrooms include a heterogeneous group of students with very different sets of skills and abilities.

One of the questions often asked of us in the course of sharing an inquiry-based lesson with educators is "How can we use an inquiry lesson in a classroom that has many mixed-ability students and/or underserved learners?" The heart of the answer of course is how you, the classroom teacher, can modify the inquiry lesson model so that it meets the learning needs of all students while not compromising the integrity of the lesson. This section of the chapter will present interventions that teachers, co-teachers, and teaching assistants can use to assist those students who will find the inquiry lesson challenging.

In essence, how can we prepare students for the ILM lesson format, and what differentiation strategies would become most effective for teaching this particular lesson with these particular students? We have included a set of graphic organizers that have been designed and field-tested by the authors in their secondary and university classrooms. Younger students or students who are new to the ILM format tend to benefit more from the structure provided by the graphic organizers. Students with learning challenges also often appreciate the sense of unity and organization of thought provided by the graphic organizers.

Teachers can also scaffold the material in ways that may work for their specific students for a particular class. If you are using these lessons in a higher-education setting, you may find you need only verbalize much of the structure held within these graphic organizers, or perhaps use them the first time you implement an ILM lesson in your classroom. We encourage you to think critically about the graphic organizers and use or modify them to suit your teaching situation and/or style. They are valuable tools for learning, cognitive scaffolding, and classroom management, but only if they are tailored to your specific learning setting.

DIFFERENTIATED STRATEGIES FOR DIVERSE LEARNERS

Since learners in classrooms today are more diverse than ever, it is completely understandable that we need to differentiate the ways in which we deliver our content so that all learners can benefit from the same lesson. Differentiation is best accomplished within a collaborative model. For success, it is necessary to work with colleagues to help develop specific learning strategies for your particular class or classes. Since, in the words of Tomlinson (2017), the hallmark of differentiation lies in a teacher examination of the content being delivered, the process delivering said content, and the products desired of students to illustrate mastery of the material, it is imperative that the teacher review the inquiry lesson for several points.

First, what are the readiness levels of your students for this type of lesson? What challenge will you need to address in using this model? Second, what are the interests of the students in this particular topic (or conversely, how will you develop high interest?)? And third, considering the learning profile of your students, what modifications and/or accommodations will need to be made to your use of the ILM for this lesson? Once the teacher has considered these points in terms of the learning objectives, it would be appropriate to begin planning for the ILM lesson with students.

Again, by using the ILM, the teacher is deliberately encouraging increased motivation and engagement with all students, especially those who might consider themselves not interested in participation and formal engagement. The following is a list of potential strategies that can be effectively employed within the framework of the lessons included here in this text. Remember, this list is not exhaustive.

1. Use of graphic organizers to aid students in thinking about (scaffolding of thinking), recording (memorializing the thinking into coherent pieces), and organizing facts (summative work) in the ILM lesson format (tailored to meet your own classroom needs as necessary).
2. Summarized article "talking points" that will help with reading comprehension of new material, background knowledge to "jump into" the lesson ideas, and comprehension issues (pulling the learning together).

3. Use of an evaluation and reflection worksheet for students to integrate their respective thoughts on the lesson, as well as reflect upon the effectiveness of their group interactions.

By utilizing these strategies, you will be able to reach a much wider audience of students who may need assistance to complete each task in an ILM lesson. Additionally, they can be used to encourage a self-reflective practice or learning style that will greatly enhance participation and self-guided discovery. Often, in reviewing the reflective nature of the evaluation worksheets, teachers can and will be better prepared to generate future ILM lessons for their particular set of students.

THE ROLE OF PRIOR KNOWLEDGE

As educators, we all recognize the value that background knowledge plays in student engagement, the processing of new information, and ultimately academic success. Working with students who have difficulties in grasping new content material, it has always been a successful strategy to review new material before they will see it in the general classroom. Teaching with the ILM challenges this notion. In fact, ILM lessons have repeatedly demonstrated academic success and typically do not require such knowledge in order to arrive at the answer to the focus question. The focus question helps to maintain the overall goal of the lesson for the students in the classroom.

For students with significant learning barriers, however, you may decide that it might be important for them to review some of the basic tenets of the lesson—without, of course, giving away to them the answer to the focus question of the lesson. You may decide that it is appropriate to provide some additional vocabulary words at the beginning of the lesson(s). You may decide that it would be beneficial to review some important people depending upon your lesson, for example.

Remember, it is more important to guard the integrity of the focus question than it is to preteach some of the material within the lesson. Your best judgment is most appropriate in making decisions about preteaching some material of the lesson for students with learning barriers.

USING THINKING STRATEGIES

The use of thinking strategies is also critically important if students are to benefit from an inquiry model lesson. As teachers, we are always striving to achieve content mastery for all our students—regardless of ability level.

Thinking strategies (or scaffolding of the thinking) will enable and support underserved learners in achieving a higher level of content mastery and participation similar to their regular classmates.

Art educator Philip Yenawine (1999) developed a set of questioning techniques that has helped many students achieve a higher level of content and lesson knowledge while studying art at museums and in schools across the country. Called visual thinking skills, these strategies can be helpful by assisting students in the scaffolding process of thinking about what they are looking at and developing ideas and questions.

Since the ILM lesson requires analysis of multiple prompts (a picture, a document, an artifact, a video clip, etc.), any strategy that assists in students' development of critical thinking and questioning will be very helpful. Students who struggle with processing and connecting new information typically benefit from thinking strategies, especially in an ILM lesson. It is important to note that as the teacher considers their class and the class's needs for learning the new material, many of these strategies could prove instructive for the whole class, not just a particular group of students. Again, this can be adjusted depending upon the ILM lesson and the learning objectives that the teacher has selected.

The teacher or co-teacher (or teaching assistant) can often lead or scaffold the learning and thinking process of a single homogenous or heterogenous grouping of students by using the thinking strategies mentioned above. At the introduction of a prompt or picture in an ILM lesson, the following verbal scaffolds can be very helpful:

- Let's take a moment to look carefully at this (picture, etc.); what do you see?
- What is happening in this picture? What "action" do you see?
- What do you see that makes you say that?
- What more can we find, especially when adding this to our other prompts?

Summarize students' responses using conditional language ("Jaquan and now Abby think this could be . . ."). This keeps the conversation open to other interpretations by other students. If appropriate, ask, "What do you see that makes you say that?" This encourages students to back up their statements with things they see. Using these thinking prompts, teachers can help groups of students scaffold their thinking to assist in the critical analysis of the prompts.

We must be sure we as teachers do not provide the core part of the input to the ILM—it's student thinking that is important here. Scaffolding questions that assist student thinking about the overall focus question and how these visual thinking strategies can assist students in their deliberation of a prompt that relates to the focus question is the heart of our differentiation assistance.

GRAPHIC ORGANIZERS

As outlined above, several generic graphic organizers are available on the authors' website (see introduction for web address). Again, they are meant to be modified based on what you have developed for your own ILM lessons.

1. Lesson Guidelines: This organizer represents the guidelines we have come to rely on when implementing an ILM lesson. This version of the guidelines is useful to project or hang somewhere in the room; or as was suggested, you might laminate it and leave it with each group during a lesson. Use this organizer in step 2 of the lesson.

   Lesson Guidelines
   - Your group will have 5–8 minutes to analyze each artifact you receive.
   - Your group will only receive one artifact at a time; you must share the artifact with everyone in your group.
   - As a group, you need to develop several questions about the artifact. Keep in mind you are trying to answer the question introduced at the beginning of class.
   - Your question must be phrased in such a way that it is answerable with a *yes* or *no*. Remember that questions answered with a no may be just as valuable as questions answered with a *yes*.
   - Your group may only ask one question per round.
   - You need to assign two note takers. The first note taker will write down the questions the group brainstorms. The second note taker will write down all the questions and answers asked by the other groups.
   - Pay close attention! Other groups' questions will not be repeated.
   - While analyzing artifacts, speak softly so that your conversation is only heard by your group members.
   - Your ultimate goal is to connect the clues together to answer the question presented at the beginning of class.

2. Lesson Guidelines with Roles and Contract: This graphic organizer has the guidelines along with a signup sheet for the different roles students assume during an ILM lesson. It also has a space for students to sign their names, pledging to do their best to follow the guidelines required by the lesson. Our advice is to have students read and sign this document at the outset of the lesson, during step 2, see chapter 3 for details. Ask students

to refer back to it when students complete the Evaluation and Reflection worksheet.

Student Roles:
- Recorders: responsible for recording the group's questions and answers and the questions and answers from other groups.
- Theory writer: responsible for leading the group as it develops a theory to answer the question asked at the beginning of class. Write the group's theory on the board.
- Timer: Keeps track of how much time the group has during each round of inquiry. Remind the group to stay focused, if necessary.
- Fact checker: Responsible for making sure all questions and theory put forward by the group align with all the data presented.

3. Yes/No Worksheets: With these graphic organizers, students can record questions on the worksheets asked both by their group and the other groups. This is necessary to help students think critically and strategically about the other groups' questions and whether each question asked is helpful in future group deliberation. Again, make adjustments here based upon the readiness and ability of the group(s).
4. Theory Worksheet: In each lesson, there is a built-in pause about halfway through the cycle of prompts. While the lessons recommend specifically where to take this pause, you should do so when you sense your students are starting to piece together a thoughtful answer to the focus question. At this point, pass out the theory statement worksheet and ask groups to spend a few minutes formulating a one-sentence answer to the focus question. Invite the theory writer to put their group's statement on the board. Once they have done so, review each statement and highlight accuracies (as well as inaccuracies) in their theories. Use this as an opportunity to begin to steer them in the correct direction based on the prompts remaining in the lesson, if needed.
5. Evaluation and Reflection Worksheet: This graphic organizer is used at the end of the lesson during step 7. This last step is easy to skip, but we strongly encourage you to complete it—particularly if you plan to do another ILM lesson in the future. Giving the students the chance to evaluate their learning, skill building, and behavior significantly increases the likelihood that they will remember the material taught in the lesson, improve their critical thinking skills, and increase their understanding of what it means to collaborate. See chapter 3 for more on step 7.
6. Ticket Out the Door: This graphic organizer can be used in lieu of the summary asked for at the bottom of the Evaluation and Reflection Worksheet. It is a much faster way to assess the effectiveness of the

lesson. Typically, students are provided the Ticket Out the Door when there are only a few minutes left in the class. They complete the questions asked and hand the ticket to the teacher on their way out the door. If you want to use the ticket as a grade, you will want the students to put their names at the top. If you are using the ticket to evaluate the effectiveness of the lesson, and not necessarily individual students' understanding, you can ask students to leave their names off the ticket. This type of formative assessment can be critical in determining whether your students understand the concepts from the lesson. Additionally, it could also be useful to the teacher in understanding how well the students were doing in the thinking and deliberating parts of the inquiry lesson.

We have developed a model of instruction that increases student engagement and student learning. By utilizing this student-centered model, you can develop lessons that will spark engagement, cognitive interdependence, and cooperation. The ILM can be used across a wide variety of subject disciplines and can be used and adjusted by the classroom teacher to fit their subject needs. Differentiation of the model and its teaching is easily accomplished by using strategies outlined above, or as we have noted, through the lens of the teacher considering the content, process, and products needed at the end of the lesson. The ILM is one that has universal application and has proven to be effective in raising student engagement and student learning.

INQUIRY LEARNING MODEL—DIFFERENTIATED STRATEGIES FOR LESSON 4, EXPLOITATION AND IMMORTALITY: THE STORY OF HENRIETTA LACKS

We have included in this chapter some differentiated strategies that we have found to be helpful in working with students who struggle with the inquiry model and/or the content of the lesson. The suggestions include key vocabulary and learning objectives, differentiation of the prompts used in the lesson, and finally, the use of thinking strategies, as explained above, to assist students in the deduction process in support of their thinking about the central focus question. Of course, development of a different scaffold for instruction is always encouraged based upon your content, lesson, and learning outcomes for students. Creativity is key!

Differentiation of Prompts

So, our focus question was this: Whose cells are they? How, then, can we use "differentiation" with this lesson, and how can we use prompts that appeal to the different intelligences of our classrooms? Let's take a look at the prompts we have established with the idea of using possible accommodations thinking about the visual, auditory, kinesthetic, or tactile learning channels (see following table):

Prompt #	Description	Possible additional prompts (think possible visual, auditory, kinesthetic, tactile additions)
1	Picture of H. Lacks	Pictures from childhood
2	Photograph of "HeLa" cells	Microscope, various photos "HeLa" cells
3	Excerpt on Dr. Gey and photo from Rebecca Skloot book	Photos of Johns Hopkins, photo of "Colored Only" door
4	Lyrics of song by Helen Lane, "Helen Lacks," from YouTube	
5	Chart—Cases of polio, 1940–2000	Contributions to other diseases and scientific research. Photograph of Salk, photographs of kids with polio
6	Lacks's historical marker; photo of H. Lacks's gravestone	
7	Article on impact of HeLa cells in *Huffington Post*	News reports of updates on family, photographs of Lacks family today

The accommodations in the preceding table are not offered as the "best" way to differentiate, because, as stated, you as the teacher are the expert in deciding which way to use the inquiry lesson to work with your particular students.

Scaffolding for Thinking about Prompts

The strategy we introduce here for this lesson is student-centered learning and differentiation. The use of visual thinking skills (Yenawine, 1999) can often be helpful to assist in this scaffolding process for your students who have learning barriers. At the addition of an input, the teacher, co-teacher, or teaching assistant can often try to lead the learning and thinking process for a specific group by using the following:

- Let's take a moment to look carefully at this (picture, etc.); what do you see?
- What is happening in this picture? What "action" do you see?
- What do you see that makes you say that?
- What more can we find, especially when adding this to our other prompts?

Using these thinking prompts, often teachers can help groups of students with the scaffolding of their thinking to assist in the critical analysis of the prompts. We must be sure, however, that we *do not* provide the core part of the input—it's the thinking that is important here. Scaffolding questions that assist thinking about the overall focus question and how these visual thinking strategies assist students in arriving at the essential junction between their thinking/analysis of the prompts provided and the focus question.

Differentiated Graphic Organizer

The graphic organizer included is meant to be used with a group of students that may have some significant learning struggles in the classroom. It is similar to our general graphic organizer (chapter 3), except here we have done some of the thinking for them. For example, we provide a text box for the students to summarize the information from the prompt.

Additionally, there is in the background a "thinking" graphic with gears meant to help students, that, while the prompts are important, it's the thinking and subsequent linkage of all of the prompts to assist and support them in trying to answer the central focus question: Who do these cells belong to? It will also assist them in thinking about and then develop a yes or no question asked between rounds of the prompts.

CONCLUSION

It is our hope that the suggestions provided above will assist you and your colleagues in delivering a successful inquiry lesson with your students. While inquiry is an excellent way to assist students in discovering and learning about different points in history, the lesson at times may prove a challenge with some of your students. By using some of the ideas presented here, we are confident that you will be able to use the inquiry lesson with a very diverse group of students. Refer to the authors' website for downloadable copies of all the graphic organizers and prompts referenced in this chapter. A link to the authors' website may be found in the introduction.

PART II

Lessons

What follows are six ILM lesson examples across various disciplines, including mathematics, history, science, English as a new language, and Chinese as a foreign language. The sample lessons were designed to help teachers get started with the ILM and to assist teachers who wish to design their own ILM lessons. Each of the six sample lessons follow the ILM format and include teacher background information. Each sample lesson also includes prompts that can be used when executing the lesson. The prompts are available on the authors website at www.inquirylearningmodel.com. Instructional videos on the ILM and related content are also available on the website.

Chapter 5

Lesson 1: The Disappearing Aral Sea (History/Earth Science)

This lesson may be situated in any of several units of instruction. You may choose to focus on a particular theme (e.g., Soviet history, Cold War politics, geography, contemporary geopolitics, or human-made environmental crises) in a humanities classroom. The lesson is also adaptable to a geography or earth science classroom (see Science Connections to This Lesson at the end of the chapter).

BACKGROUND INFORMATION FOR THE TEACHER

The Aral Sea crisis started during the Soviet era with Joseph Stalin's sweeping agricultural reforms and continued with Nikita Khrushchev's decision to increase agricultural production. As a result, the Aral Sea, which regional populations once depended upon heavily, became an ecological, political, and economic disaster. Prior to the 1960s, the Aral Sea was the fourth largest lake in the world, as measured by surface area, only behind the Caspian Sea, Lake Superior, and Lake Victoria.

Today the Aral Sea does not even rank as one of the top 10 largest lakes in the world. This human-made disaster happened because the Aral Sea is primarily a river-fed body of water, supported by the Amu Darya and Syr Darya rivers. The water from these rivers was diverted for irrigation to support cotton and food crop production in the Central Asian desert region of the Soviet Union. Twenty years after the water from the rivers was redirected for irrigation purposes, the volume of water left in the sea was reduced by more than half.

Over time, the water remaining in the Aral Sea changed composition, becoming increasingly salty. The salinization of the water caused a steep reduction in the number of species of animals living in and around the sea, which then caused the death of the fishing industry previously supported by the sea. Also, as the water level receded, salt and other pollutants in the water became airborne, causing an increase in tuberculosis, various cancers, and other diseases among local populations.

In short, those living in the immediate vicinity of the Aral Sea in Kazakhstan and Uzbekistan have suffered health problems, loss of livelihood, loss of drinkable water, and loss of a means of growing food. This crisis was brought to the American public in a February 1990 *National Geographic* article, "A Soviet Sea Lies Dying" (Ellis and Turnley). The article provided many photographs of the receding seabed as well as of the devastation to the population, the collapsing economic infrastructure, and the declining health of the communities that formerly surrounded the seashore.

Rob Ferguson's (2003) *The Devil and the Disappearing Sea* provides a more detailed account of the economic, political, and human disaster facilitated by politicians in the former Soviet Union.

The 1990 *National Geographic* article did not, however, tell the whole story. This human-made catastrophe also involves an island in the middle of the Aral Sea, Vozrozhdeniya Island. The Soviets used the island to conduct research on biological and chemical weapons and as a storage facility for byproducts of nuclear testing. Weapons-grade anthrax and bubonic plague were researched at the facility, and the remnants of that research are still on the island today, but the island is no longer an island.

In 2001, receding water levels turned the island into a peninsula, and by 2008, when the southeast section of the former Aral Sea completely dried up, the landmass formerly identified as Vozrozhdeniya Island ceased to exist.

The location was initially selected by the Soviet military establishment as a research facility because of the natural security the island provided. Once the island became a peninsula and a part of the mainland, that natural security disappeared. Since the crisis occurred after the fall of the Soviet Union, Russia took little responsibility for securing the former research facility. The two countries bordering the Aral Sea, Kazakhstan and Uzbekistan, had little in the way of resources to clean up the research facility. Working against them were also political and economic forces that stifled international cooperation. Hence, a multifaceted, international environmental and health crisis still exists around the Aral Sea.

Key Vocabulary and Terms

Communist
Cultivation
Ecological
Peninsula
Resources
Salinization
Satellite
Semiarid
Soviet Union

Lesson 1: The Disappearing Aral Sea (History/Earth Science) 49

Lesson Plan Objectives

Skills-Based Objectives

During this lesson the students will:
- work cooperatively in small groups
- analyze primary and secondary source documents
- reconcile information from multiple prompts
- interpret information from several types of maps
- develop questions based on document analysis
- advance a theory that answers the focus question
- modify the theory as information is added

Content-Based Objectives

During this lesson the students will:
- infer consequences of centralized communist government decision-making
- recognize importance of checks and balances within a political system
- summarize environmental dangers of poor resource management

Focus Question

The focus question for this lesson might sound unconventional, but after several field tests with the material, it seems to be the question that best ignites student interest. The question is, "So what? Why should I care?" Teachers could also ask, "What is going on here?" or simply, "What happened?" Often the question you decide upon will be dependent on the thematic focus you select for the lesson.

Procedures

Please refer to chapter 3 for detailed instructions regarding the setup and steps for an ILM lesson. Prior to the start of class, remember to arrange your prompts (duplicate for the numbers of student groups you have) in a location that is easy for you to access, but also separate from your students. Select your groups (three or four students in a group ideally) and arrange desks to facilitate group interaction. Write the focus question "So what? Why should I care?" on the board.

Step 1: Investigate and Prepare

This step has been completed for you. Be familiar with the background information above so that you are knowledgeable and prepared to answer any questions that the students will ask.

Step 2: Introduce Focus Question

At the beginning of class, settle the students into their groups and explain the guidelines of the mystery game they are about to play (see chapter 3 for details). Provide each group with one copy of the guidelines at the outset. You might even want your students to sign a pledge that they will endeavor to follow the guidelines. Introduce the focus question for the day and proceed directly with the first prompt.

Step 3: Start Questioning Rounds

The next segment of class will be devoted to students' analysis of the various prompts required for the lesson. The first prompt for this lesson is the photograph of the fishing boats stranded in the dried-up seabed of the Aral Sea.

Prompt 1: National Geographic Photo of Aral Sea

It is a compelling photo that instantly engages students and promotes divergent thinking. Give students a specific amount of time to talk in their groups about the prompt. During this time, usually 5–8 minutes, the students must prepare two or more questions to ask you. Remember to remind the students that the questions must be asked in such a way as to be answerable with a yes or a no.

Circulate among the groups and listen to the questions the students are developing. You might find that calling on groups in a particular order based on their questions is beneficial to the class's accumulated understanding of the mystery they are trying to solve.

When the analysis round time is up, invite the students to raise their hands to ask you their group's question. Be sure to insist that the question they ask is answerable with a yes or a no. Review the steps to the model in chapter 3 for clarification. Give each group the opportunity to ask their question, ensuring that the class can hear both the questions and the answers.

Encourage the students to take notes on the facts that are being accumulated by the questions. As you will see, there is a decided advantage for those students who listen carefully to the questions posed by other groups. When students listen to the answers provided by the teacher and process the information generated by their classmates' questions, they may change or hone their own questions. Encouraging students to listen carefully to the other groups also acts as an effective classroom management strategy.

Once the first questioning round is complete, proceed in this manner with the next several prompts. You may choose to rotate which group begins the

Lesson 1: The Disappearing Aral Sea (History/Earth Science) 51

Source: David Turnley, used with permission

questioning for each round so that the same group does not ask the first question in every round.

Prompt 2: Bag of Salt

Because this prompt is tactile in nature, it will immediately grab students' attention. It is not uncommon for students to ask if they can smell, or even taste, the substance in the bag. Be sure to caution them to use the same rules they might use in a science lab when encountering an unknown substance. In the questions for this round, a group will inevitably ask the obvious question, "Is this salt?" While a basic question, the role that salt plays in the ecological disaster is central to understanding the Aral Sea crisis.

This prompt can sometimes foster misconceptions as students immediately think the sea was drained for salt mining. That misconception can be easily addressed when a group asks that question. The answer then leaves students wondering about the significance of the salt and how it relates to the larger question at hand.

There is an image of a hand holding salt on the authors' website for your use. This image is particularly helpful if you are conducting the ILM virtually. If you are in person, however, it is recommended that you fill Ziplock bags with roughly one-half cup of salt (rock salt is preferable, if available). In field tests, this more tactile prompt engaged students in the questioning round more strongly than did the image.

Prompt 3: Map of Agricultural Areas and Principal Crops of Kazakhstan

This prompt allows students to narrow down the geographic area related to the lesson. Questions asking if the boats from prompt 1 are near the Caspian, Black, or other sea on the map are often asked until students determine that the ships were near the Aral Sea. Once this fact is uncovered, students can then analyze the land usage around the sea using this map. This image is available on the authors' website. (See the introduction for a link.)

Prompt 4: Hand Holding Sand

This prompt is used to add a layer of complexity to the lesson. Once the sea dried up, the resultant sand became airborne. This spread vast amounts of pesticides and other chemicals, which caused many health problems such as tuberculosis and birth defects. These health problems further exacerbated the economic and social crisis experienced by the residents surrounding the Aral Sea. As was the case with the bag of salt, it is recommended that you pass out bags with sand in them to each group if teaching the lesson in person. If you are teaching the lesson virtually, a photo of a hand holding sand is available on the authors' website. (See the introduction for a link to the website.)

Prompt 5: Maps of the Aral Sea over Time

This prompt moves students' understanding of the problem forward significantly. An analysis of the satellite images and maps reveals the shrinkage of the sea over time. The implications of this shrinkage are evident even to younger students. It is during this round that students start to theorize that actions taken by humankind caused the disaster to happen. This image is available for download on the authors' webpage. See the introduction for the website address.

Step 4: Unveil Working Theories

At a point in the questioning rounds, when you sense your students are homing in on a possible answer to the focus question, pause. With this lesson

Lesson 1: The Disappearing Aral Sea (History/Earth Science) 53

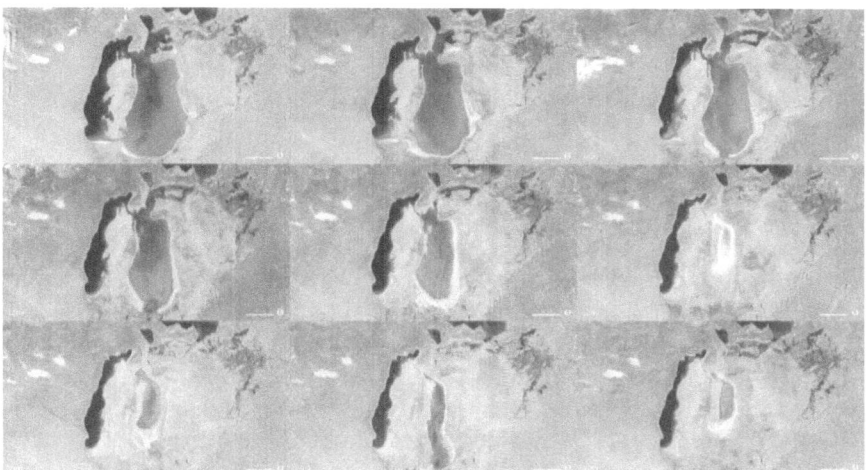

Source: NASA Earth Observatory

field tests indicated that this pause was usually most effective after prompt 5. Ask each group to craft one sentence, or a theory statement, that sums up their response to the focus question. As you circulate around the room, assist students with wording, challenge their assumptions, and ask for evidence as they work on this task. This process typically takes about 10 minutes, but the amount of time may vary depending on the skill level of the students.

As groups finish composing their sentences, invite one person from each group to write their response on the board. You can take this opportunity to assess the entire class for misconceptions, misinterpretations, and general understanding. As students see other groups' theories on the board, it may help advance their own thinking. This is especially helpful in classrooms that are heterogeneously grouped. A graphic organizer is provided on the authors' website that you may use to assist students in the crafting of their theory statement. (See introduction for the website address.) If this lesson is taught using a virtual platform, students may post their theories using Jamboard or another similar whiteboard software so that all of the students may read through them. This type of platform also provides the teacher with the opportunity to comment on and even edit student theories.

Once all the groups have written theories on the board, review them for accuracy. Be cautious not to overly criticize a theory that is far off the mark. The theory is, after all, the students' best working idea at the time. Highlight the theories that come close to summing up the situation under study, and encourage students to use those theories in their thinking.

54   Chapter 5

Step 5: Investigate Remaining Prompts

Resume with the remaining prompts and questioning rounds until all the prompts have been distributed.

Prompt 6: Environmental Problems of the Former Soviet Union Map

This two-part prompt is designed to introduce a new element into the mystery of the Aral Sea crisis—the biological and chemical weapons testing. The article, "Lesson in Environmental Degradation," is by E. D. Boyle (2000). During this round, students tend to struggle to reconcile the environmental disaster they are just beginning to grasp with the new information about weapons testing provided by the map and article. (This biological and chemical weapons testing map is available on the authors' webpage.)

Source: GRID-Arendal

It is recommended that a reading accompany this prompt. Note that when giving students articles to read, it is important to keep them as brief as possible. Also, since all the students need to read the article in order to participate, we recommend providing a copy for each student. This is true for the next two prompts, as well. The article is available for your use on the authors' webpage. (See the introduction for a link.)

Prompt 7: Washington Report on Middle East Affairs
Article by Lucy Jones (1999)

This prompt ties together the various facets of the Aral Sea crisis for the students. You will hear lots of "oohs" and "ahs" during this round and the next as students begin to connect all of their facts to discern a human-made environmental disaster. As is the case with the other prompts, this article is available on the authors' webpage.

Prompt 8: Discovery News *Article by Antoine Lambroschini*

This article from *Discovery News* titled "Aral Sea Revived by Dam" is written by Antoine Lambroschini (2008). Like prompt 7, this article helps students tie together the prompts they have accumulated into a cohesive story. This article is available for download on the authors' webpage. If time is short, prompts 7 and 8 can be given at the same time.

Prompt 9: Link to NPR News Story on the Revival of the Aral Sea

The last prompt is a link to a news broadcast produced by National Public Radio (NPR) in the United States. The broadcast is entitled, *Dam Revives Aral Sea and Nearby Communities*, and was first aired on Morning Edition, on October 1, 2007. It summarizes the Aral Sea crisis and provides closure for many of the students' questions. It is a good idea to close with prompts like this one so that students are able to tie all of the detailed information they just learned together. (Follow this link to the broadcast: https://www.commonlit.org/en/texts/dam-revives-aral-sea-nearby-communities-in-kazakhstan)

Step 6: Revise Theories and Discuss

Ask students to revisit their theory statement and make modifications based on their more developed understanding of the problem presented. Depending on time remaining, invite one to three groups to present their statements in answer to the focus question. Use their work as a jumping-off point to discuss the Aral Sea crisis. It is at this point when you can invite the students to openly ask you questions about the topic and you can freely fill in the gaps in their understanding.

Step 7: Evaluate and Reflect

The last step in this lesson is to ask students to evaluate and reflect on their learning. This can be done using the Evaluation and Reflection Worksheet referenced chapter 4. (A sample Evaluation and Reflection Worksheet is shared in the authors' webpage. See the introduction for a link to that webpage.) The Aral Sea lesson is flexible in that the focus can be placed on many different aspects of the crisis—geography, politics, Soviet history, environmental disaster, and so forth. The evaluation should focus on the specific learning objectives targeted for the students.

Note, when you reproduce these resources for your ILM lesson, be careful not to copy the caption. Providing students with the captions will give them more information than is necessary in the lesson.

Science Connections to This Lesson

In addition to exploring political and environmental issues that make this lesson valuable in a world history classroom, this lesson may be used in a science classroom. It is a case study for resource depletion and the negative impact humans have on the ecosystem in an environmental science classroom. You may consider collaborating with a science teacher and align this social studies lesson with a science lesson that complements the scientific aspects of this topic. In the earth science classroom, it may help to explain the rock cycle and the study of minerals.

The Aral Sea lesson provides teachers with the opportunity to address a common misconception among students studying geology. They typically don't understand that rock salt deposits—such as those found in the Aral Sea basin—are produced by the evaporation of seawater over time. This process was going on long before the crisis came to the forefront, for thousands of years. The drop in the level of the Aral Sea has exposed these salt beds but has not caused the presence of the salt deposits. Evaporation of seawater is a natural part of the rock cycle, which deposits rock that is classified as crystalline sedimentary.

Students typically have some difficulty distinguishing between the three different types of sedimentary rocks. While their understanding of clastic sedimentary rocks—those formed from rock fragments of varying size—is typically good, the subtle but important distinction of crystalline sedimentary is not well understood. Many students take away from a unit on the rock cycle that sedimentary rocks are dull (in luster), earthy, and noncrystalline. The

Lesson 1: The Disappearing Aral Sea (History/Earth Science)

rock salt samples clearly show that this is a crystalline rock. Many students would misclassify this rock as igneous due to the crystals.

Igneous rocks tend to be crystalline because they form from melted rock that crystallizes as it cools. Crystalline sedimentary rocks are crystalline because the dissolved minerals form crystals as the water evaporates. The Aral Sea lesson provides an excellent opportunity to "solidify," if you will, a crucial concept in earth science and to deepen students' understanding of the rock cycle, which is foundational in the study of the Earth.

Additionally, the rock salt is composed of the single mineral halite. Halite has a unique set of properties that students in earth science could use to identify it. It would be instructive to provide the students with a table of mineral properties and allow the students an opportunity to determine these properties. For halite, its glassy luster, relatively low hardness on the Mohs scale, and most importantly, its cubic cleavage are easily determined. No other common minerals have these three properties in common with halite. If the students are taking earth science concurrently, asking them to identify the halite would support their earth science learning as well.

A study of a topographic map of the Aral Sea area in coordination with an earth science teacher would provide another opportunity for students to see the Aral Sea on a map. Students typically enrolled in an earth science class are at the beginning stages of being able to reason spatially. There is generally not adequate time in an earth science course to provide students with enough opportunities to interact with maps until they can visualize the land in three dimensions. This is a very big step for learners in early to mid-adolescence. In the case of the Aral Sea, the topography is such that it is a basin shape with no place for an outlet. This fact would show up by comparing its map to a map of another lake, such as Lake George in upstate New York, which does have an outlet. Deducing this from a study of the isolines would be excellent spatial practice for students.

Chapter 6

Lesson 2: Let's Travel to an English-Speaking City (World Languages/TESOL)

BACKGROUND INFORMATION FOR THE TEACHER

This inquiry lesson fully immerses English language (EL) students in the English language in determining the destination to which they will be traveling. The intent is for students to use context clues, both written and pictorial, to figure out the city they will visit. A series of We Chat messages, along with artifacts, will assist the students in their quest to learn where they will be going. They will be utilizing geographical and cultural knowledge along with fluency of their English-language skills.

As the students encounter each artifact, they will need to use critical thinking skills to make educated guesses about their destination, eventually homing in on the target city of Sydney, Australia. This lesson is designed for travelers originating in Beijing, China. You may select another departure and/or arrival city to best meet the needs of your students and your curriculum.

Key Vocabulary and Terms

Architectural wonder	Geography
Architecture	Marsupials
Boarding pass	Opera
Culture	Passport
Currency	Packing list
Destination	Universal travel adapter

Lesson Plan Objectives
Skills-Based Objectives
During this lesson the students will:
- work cooperatively in small groups
- analyze primary and secondary source documents
- reconcile information from multiple prompts
- interpret information from several different types of prompts
- develop questions based on document analysis
- advance a theory that answers the focus question
- modify the theory as information is added

Content-Based Objectives
During this lesson the students will:
- infer travel plans based on evidence presented
- recognize important cultural sites of Sydney, Australia
- summarize travel plans in English

Focus Question

As is the case with many focus questions in the ILM, it is deceptively simple: Where are we going? In field research, we have found that questions need to combine intrigue with vagueness. A question that is too detailed gives the students too much information, whereas a more general question challenges them to figure out the mystery being presented. "Where are we going?" achieves the best results with this lesson.

Procedures

Please refer to chapter 3 for detailed instructions regarding the setup and steps for an ILM Lesson. Prior to the start of class, remember to arrange your prompts (duplicate for the numbers of student groups you have) in a location that is easy for you to access, but also separate from your students. Select your groups (three or four students in a group ideally) and arrange desks to facilitate group interaction. Write the focus question "Where are we going?" on the board.

Step 1: Investigate and Prepare

This step has been completed for you. Become familiar with the background information so you are knowledgeable and prepared to answer questions that the students will ask.

Step 2: Introduce Focus Question

At the beginning of class, settle the students into their groups and explain the guidelines (see chapter 3 for details). Provide each group with one copy of the guidelines at the outset. Have them sign the pledge that they will endeavor to follow the guidelines. Introduce the focus question for the day and proceed directly to the first prompt.

Step 3: Start Questioning Rounds

The next segment of class will be devoted to students' analysis of the various prompts required for the lesson. The first prompt of this lesson is a We Chat exchange between them and a friend. The message shows that the friend is planning a surprise trip, giving only the clues of "famous city" and "architectural wonder." Give students a specific time to talk about the text. During this time, usually about three minutes, the students must prepare two or more questions to ask you.

Circulate among the groups and listen to the questions that the students are developing. You might find that calling on groups in a particular order based on their questions is beneficial to the accumulated understanding of the mystery the students are trying to solve.

Prompt 1: We Chat between Me and Friend, #1

In prompt 1, students read a message exchange between two friends. The friend is asked to go on a trip, agrees, and quickly decides to plan the trip as a surprise to the sender. In the message, the friend drops two clues for the students: that it will be to a famous city and that it has an architectural wonder. Perhaps students will begin brainstorming architectural wonders, such as the seven wonders of the world, which may focus them on many different cities around the globe. (An image of this We Chat is available for download on the authors' website; see the introduction for the link.)

When the analysis round time is up, invite the students to raise their hands and ask you their group's question. Be sure to insist that the question is answerable with a yes or a no. Review the steps in chapter 3 for clarification. Give each group the opportunity to ask its question, ensuring that the class can hear both the question and the answers. Encourage the students to take notes on the facts that the questions accumulate.

As you will see, there is a decided advantage for those students who listen carefully to the questions the other groups pose. When students listen to the answers the teacher provides and process the information their classmates' questions generate, they may change or refine their own questions.

62   Chapter 6

Encouraging students to listen carefully to the other groups also acts as an effective classroom management strategy.

Once the first questioning round is complete, continue in this manner with the next several prompts. You may choose to rotate which group begins the questioning for each round, so that the same group does not as the first question in every round.

Prompt 2: Airplane Boarding Pass, Passport, and English Translator

Prompt 2 shows three images. The first is a boarding pass from Beijing to an unknown destination, approximately a 12-hour flight, in the month of July. The second is of a Chinese passport, and the third, a picture of an app for an English dictionary. Students can use these clues to determine that they will be traveling abroad to an English-speaking city in the month of July.

(An image of this We Chat is available for download on the authors' website; see the introduction for the link.)

Prompt 3: We Chat between Me and Friend, #2

Prompt 3 is a second We Chat message from the friend, suggesting that entertainment is brought on board the airplane, as the flight will last more than ten hours. In addition, our friend reminds us to convert our money to dollars. (An image of this We Chat is available for download on the authors' website; see the introduction for the link.)

Prompt 4: Pictures of Australian Currency and Sydney Rail Central Station

Prompt 4 shows currency in different denominations. This picture makes clear that the destination is not in the United States. In addition, a picture of the Central Rail Station in Sydney is presented. Students may think this is in London, especially in conjunction with a partial image of Queen Elizabeth on the $20 currency. (An image of the currency and the Sydney Rail Station is available for download on the authors' website; see the introduction for the link.)

Step 4: Unveil Working Theories

At some point in the questioning rounds, when you sense your students are homing in on a possible focus question answer, you will want to pause. With this lesson, field tests indicated that this pause was usually most effective after prompts 3 and 4. Ask each group to craft one sentence, or a theory

Lesson 2: Let's Travel to an English-Speaking City (World Languages/TESOL) 63

Source: www.freepik.com

Source: https://commons.wikimedia.org/wiki/File:Sydney_Central_Railway_Station.jpg

statement, that sums up their response to the focus question. As you circulate around the room, assist students with wording, challenge their assumptions, and ask for evidence as they work on this task. This process typically takes about 10 minutes, but the amount of time may vary depending on the skill level of the students.

As groups finish composing their sentences, invite one person from each group to write their response on the board. You can take this opportunity to assess the entire class for misconceptions, misinterpretations, and general understanding. As students see other groups' theories on the board, it may help advance their own thinking. This is especially helpful in classrooms that are heterogeneously grouped. A graphic organizer is provided on the authors' webpage to assist students in the crafting of their theory statements.

Once the groups have written theories on the board, review them for accuracy. Be cautious not to overly criticize a theory that is far off the mark. The theory is, after all, the students' best working ideas. Highlight the theories that come close to summing up the situation under study, and encourage students to use those theories in their thinking

Step 5: Investigate Remaining Prompts

Resume with the remaining prompts and questioning rounds until all the prompts have been distributed.

Prompt 5: We Chat between Me and Friend, #3

Prompt 5 is another message exchange with our friend. We learn that our destination is not a capital city, which rules out London. (An image of this We Chat is available for download on the authors' website; see the introduction for the link.)

Prompt 6: Packing List

Prompt 6 outlines a list of what you need to pack to take along on your trip. Reading through this list gives students an opportunity to think more about their destination as well as revisiting some preliminary English vocabulary words. What should stand out the most about this list is that it calls for warm clothing, suggesting low temperatures for the city they are visiting in July. This list is available for download on the authors' webpage.

Comb	Boots	Books
Dental floss	Gloves	Camera
Deodorant	Long-sleeved shirts	Downloaded movie
Hairbrush	Pants	Charger
Razor	Scarf	English translator
Shampoo	Socks	Local currency
Soap	Sweater	Passport/identification
Toothbrush	Underwear	Phone
Toothpaste	Winter coat	Universal travel adapter

Lesson 2: Let's Travel to an English-Speaking City (World Languages/TESOL) 65

Prompt 7: We Chat between Me and Friend, #4

Prompt 7 is another message from our friend who gives some more specific clues about our destination. We learn that we are going to visit a zoo, which features marsupials. This higher-level vocabulary word, if known to students, may allow them to guess that we are going to Australia. Perhaps they will also guess that the city is Sydney. (An image of this We Chat is available for download on the authors' website; see the introduction for the link.)

Prompt 8: Photograph of the Sydney Opera House

Prompt 8 features a close-up of the architectural wonder, the Sydney Opera House, which may be immediately recognizable to some students. (An image of the Sydney Opera House is available for download on the authors' website; see the introduction for the link.)

Step 6: Revise Theories and Discuss

Ask students to revisit their theory statements and make modifications based on their more-developed understanding of the problem presented. Depending on time remaining, invite one to three groups to present their statements in answer to the focus question. Use their work as a jumping off point to discuss how they were able to figure out their travel destination. It is at this point that you can invite the students to openly ask you questions about Sydney, Australia, and you can freely fill in their gaps in understanding.

Step 7: Evaluate and Reflect

The last step in this lesson is to ask students to evaluate and reflect on their learning. This can be done using the Individual Evaluation and Reflection Worksheet. The English Destination lesson is flexible in that the focus can be placed on many different aspects of travel: geography, cultural places of interest, weather, numeracy, and literacy. The evaluation should focus on the specific learning objectives targeted for the students.

Chapter 7

Lesson 3: Cyclical Modeling
Developing Wave Phenomena (STEM)

Unlike the Inquiry Learning Model lessons in the humanities, which focus on more open-ended questions, science and mathematics lessons that utilize Inquiry Learning Lessons are designed to lead students to discover fundamental scientific or mathematical concepts.

In this lesson, students through their mathematical learning develop strategies to model situations and problems to mathematical equations. Most commonly, students have developed linear, exponential, and quadratic models. All of these mathematical models are unbounded and approach infinity or in the case of exponential decay, approach a single value.

However, many physical phenomena are cyclical in nature and it is important that students are not only able to model these situations but understand the components of the model—amplitude, period, frequency, and midline. This lesson fits naturally after the development of the unit circle. Instead of deriving the standard sine wave from a table of noncontextual ordered pairs, the lesson focuses on the context and components of the wave.

Using this Inquiry Learning Lesson will allow the student to have a deeper understanding of the elements of wave functions and will allow them to apply these concepts to novel situations involving cyclical modeling.

BACKGROUND INFORMATION FOR THE TEACHER

The word *trigonometry* is derived from Greek and means "triangle measure" and was developed in ancient Greece. This foundational mathematics focused on the common ratio of similar right triangles and the ability to utilize these ratios. Further development of trigonometric concepts was developed in China, India, and the Middle East.

Trigonometry was solely used as a geometric discipline and did not begin to transform into analytical mathematics until the 1600s. The development of the sinusoidal function on the Cartesian plane (the focus of this lesson) and standardized notation for trigonometric functions didn't develop until the late 1600s or early 1700s (Maor and Barnard 2016)

Key Vocabulary and Terms

Amplitude	Period
Cosine	Range
Cyclical	Sine
Frequency	Tangent
Maximum	Transformation
Midline	Trigonometry
Minimum	Wave

Lesson Plan Objectives

Skills-Based Objectives

During this lesson the students will:
- work cooperatively in small groups
- analyze primary and secondary source documents
- reconcile information from multiple prompts
- interpret information from several different types of prompts
- develop questions based on document analysis
- advance a theory that answers the focus question
- modify the theory as information is added

Content-Based Objectives

During this lesson the students will:
- recognize components of the wave cycle
- analyze physical phenomena and correspond them to waves
- apply wave phenomena to novel situations

Focus Question

The focus question for the lesson is "How do these relate?" This question gets at the heart of the job of a mathematician or scientist; that is, to make sense of the unknown and relate them to a mathematical model. This lesson is rich in discovering vocabulary pertaining to periodic functions.

Words like *maximums, minimums, periods* (or *cycles*), *frequency, average* (*midline*), and *range of values* are naturally developed through questioning and discussion in groups. These discussions allow students to have a complete understanding of the elements of periodic functions.

Procedures

Please refer to chapter 3 for detailed instructions regarding the setup and steps for an Inquiry Learning Lesson. Prior to class, remember to select your groups based on your students and what will be most beneficial for discussion. Heterogeneous groups of three or four tend to work best.

It is also important that you have your prompts organized and in a location that is easy for you to access but is not available for student access. Remember, it is very important that in most cases, each group is provided with only one prompt. This will promote a collaborative environment. Write the focus question, "How do these relate?" on the board. All of the images necessary for this lesson are available on the authors' website. (See the introduction for a link to that website.)

Step 1: Investigate and Prepare

This step has been completed for you. Become familiar with the background information and how each of the physical events relate to periodic models. Also become familiar how each of the elements of a sine function (i.e., amplitude, period, midline), relates to each situation. (All of the prompts are available on the authors' webpage.)

For example, using the first prompt of the London Eye, context can connect with the different elements of a wave. The maximum is the height of the Ferris wheel. The minimum is the height at which you get on the ride (not necessarily ground level because of the platform to get on). The period is the amount of time to complete one revolution and the amplitude is the length of the radius of the London Eye.

Step 2: Introduce Focus Question

At the beginning of class, settle the students into their groups and explain the guidelines (see chapter 3 for details). Provide each group with one copy of the guidelines at the onset. Have them sign the pledge that they will endeavor to follow the guidelines. Introduce the focus question for the lesson and proceed directly with the first prompt. Copies of the graphic organizers may be downloaded from that authors' webpage.

Step 3: Start Questioning Rounds

The next segment of the class will be devoted to students' analysis of the various prompts required for the lesson. The first document is a photograph of the

London Eye, but any Ferris wheel will suffice. The London Eye was erected in 1999 and is one of the world's tallest.

Prompt 1: The London Eye

The Ferris wheel is chosen specifically for the first prompt. Most students will be familiar with the amusement park ride but might not be able to relate it to mathematics. The height of a rider as the wheel traverses in a circular motion produces a cyclical function. All of the elements of the wave can be presented as described above.

Give students a specific amount of time to talk in their groups about the photograph. During this time, usually three minutes, the students should discuss the photo and prepare yes/no questions. Remind students that during the questioning period, other groups may ask one of their questions so it is important to come up with two or three questions.

During the minutes that students are analyzing the prompt, circulate among groups and listen to the questions students are developing. You might determine that calling on particular groups in a certain order might be beneficial for discovering the concept you are trying to develop. For instance, you may wish to wait to call on groups that connect the London Eye with the unit circle that you have developed in previous classes.

During this time, you may need to refocus or redirect groups if they are not on task. If students are having difficulty coming up with questions or you have a student with special needs, you may wish to prove a sentence stem for asking a question like, "Is it important that . . . " or "Does the ___ have to do with____?" Other strategies for these learnings can be used (see chapter 4: Differentiation).

When the analysis time is up, invite students to raise their hands to ask you their group's question. Be sure to insist that the question they ask is answerable with a yes or no. (For more information, review the steps in part I, chapter 2.) Give each group the opportunity to ask its question, ensuring that the class can hear both the questions and the answers. Encourage the students to take notes on the facts that the questions accumulate.

As you will see, there is a decided advantage for those students who listen carefully to the questions other groups pose. When students listen to the answers the teacher provides and process the information their classmates' questions generate, they may change or refine their own questions. Encouraging students to listen carefully to the other groups also acts as an effective classroom management strategy. (The image of the London Eye is available for download from the authors' webpage. See the introduction for a link.)

Lesson 3: Cyclical Modeling 71

Source: http://www.geograph.org.uk/photo/2429494

Once the questioning round is complete, proceed in this manner with the next three prompts. It would be beneficial to rotate which group begins the questioning for each round so that the same group does not get to ask the first question each time. In this way, it promotes listening skills and allows each group an opportunity to listen to other groups' questions and then refine their own based on the yes or no answers.

You may also notice that the students will find it easier to develop questions as the lesson progresses because there will be more prompts that they can use to look for relationships.

Prompt 2: Sound Wave Diagram

The next prompt is actually a sound wave that should be played in class. Although sound travels in longitudinal waves, it is represented graphically using traverse waves. It is an important prompt because it lends itself naturally to allow discussion of properties of waves.

The sound wave generated is a sine wave that changes in volume and frequency. Students at this point are able to pinpoint attributes of the wave but will relate it to physical representations like volume (amplitude) and pitch (frequency), but at this point will have difficulty connecting the first two prompts. This should be expected. (This image as well as the others are available for download on the authors' webpage.)

Prompt 3: A Pendulum

Prompt 3 allows students a hands-on approach to the lesson. This allows a different type of learner to become more engaged. A simple pendulum, which can be created using a weight and a piece of string, provides each group with a tangible prompt that they can explore. The pendulum allows students to gain information and students start to relate prompts 1 and 2. Vocabulary like *maximum, minimum*, and *cycles* will start to materialize. Another device that can be utilized here instead of a pendulum is a metronome if it is easily available.

Prompt 4: "The Wave" Poem

"The Wave" is a poem by an unnamed author. By now, students have a general idea that the prompts are cyclical in nature. Again, this poem attracts a different style of learning and even promotes a visual cue to a wave. When giving this prompt, you may wish to leave out the title since that gives too much information and may wish for the students to analyze the text. A website with an online tone generator may also be useful: http://onlinetonegenerator.com/.

And, a poem artistically describing characteristics of waves may be found at this website: http://charlesprize.blogspot.com/2011/10/wave.html. (An illustration of the poem is available on the authors' webpage for download.)

Step 4: Unveil Working Theories

At this point, we recommend that you pause and invite students to write a preliminary theory in answer to the focus question, "How do these relate?"

Ask each group to craft a one-sentence theory statement that sums up their response to the focus question. As you circulate around the room, assist students with wording, challenge their assumptions, and ask for evidence as they work. It is important that you remind students that their theory should be able to be supported by all the different prompts. This process usually takes about 10 minutes, but the amount of time may vary depending on the skill level of the students and their experience with inquiry.

As groups finish, invite one person from each group to write their theory statement on the board. You can take this opportunity to assess the entire class for misconceptions, misinterpretations, and general understanding. As students see other groups' theories on the board, it may help advance their own thinking. This is especially helpful in classrooms that are heterogeneously grouped. If this lesson is taught using a virtual platform, students may post their theories using Jamboard or another similar whiteboard software so that all of the students may read through them. This type of platform also provides the teacher with the opportunity to comment on and even edit student theories.

Once all the groups have written theories on the board, review them for accuracy. Be cautious not to overly criticize a theory that is far off the mark. The theory is, after all, the students' best working idea. Highlight the statements that come close to summing up the situation at play while encouraging students to dig deep into their understanding of the relationship between the prompts.

Step 5: Investigate Remaining Prompts

Return to the questioning process, using the remaining prompts. This will allow students to continue to modify their theories.

Prompt 5: Video of Waves

Using a timelapse video of tides at a location will allow students to see not only the maximums and minimums but also the cycle or period of a wave. It is important to pick a site that shows the entire cycle of the tide. This information will help students piece together amplitude (height), period, and extrema.

Depending on the video you choose, students may also note the waves in the water and make connections here as well and may even note the frequency of how the waves migrate inland. If you are unable to find a video with tides, a picture of a beach with the tide out will suffice. Here are three possible sites for useful wave videos:

- https://www.youtube.com/watch?v=1DElJu5-g-I
- https://www.youtube.com/watch?v=ynlX0umW_DA
- https://www.youtube.com/watch?v=73ADCub9AM8

Prompt 6: Temperature in Beijing Chart

Prompt 6 is a chart of the average high and low temperatures in Beijing, China, each month. One way to differentiate instruction is to provide graph paper for students to plot the data if that might encourage discussion but providing already-scaled graph paper that will help students visualize the data and saves time. Another tool to utilize is the graphing calculator if students feel comfortable creating a scatterplot.

By now, students should see the relative shape of the sine wave and should be able to make connections to prior prompts. Some groups may even attempt to sketch each of the curves for each of the prompts. (This chart is available for download on the authors' webpage. See the introduction for a link.)

Average Low and High Temperatures in Celsius by Month in Beijing, China

Month	Average high (°C)	Average low (°C)
January	1.6	−9.4
February	4.0	−6.9
March	11.3	−0.6
April	19.9	7.2
May	26.4	13.2
June	30.3	18.2
July	30.8	21.6
August	29.5	20.4
September	25.8	14.2
October	19.0	7.3
November	10.1	−0.4
December	3.3	−6.9

Prompt 7: Standing Wave Illustration

Use this prompt only if you sense that students have not quite connected the other prompts to its fullest. With one rope or metal spring toy held fixed, demonstrate different types of transverse waves. We suggest creating a standing wave where students would be able to visualize concepts like amplitude, period, frequency, maximum and minimums, and even midline.

Students might not use these vocabulary words but may use descriptions of the properties. If you choose not to utilize this prompt, proceed to the next step. You might also use this prompt later for those students that might need further reinforcement with the concept at a later time or as a formative assessment at the end of the lesson.

Step 6: Revise Theories and Discuss

Ask students to revisit their theory statements, make modifications and add more detail based on their more developed theory concentrating on the focus question, "How are these related?" Depending on the time remaining, invite one to three groups to present their theories. Use their work as a jumping-off point to discuss the connections between prompts.

At this point, you can invite students to openly ask you questions about the prompts and you can freely fill in the gaps in their understanding and introduce mathematical vocabulary they may be missing.

Step 7: Evaluate and Reflect

The last step in the lesson is to ask students to evaluate and reflect on their learning. This can be done using the Individual Evaluation and Reflection Worksheet. The ILM methodology provides students with the opportunity to take ownership of their learning. It also allows students to have contextual understanding of the components of a sine wave and will allow them to utilize a new modeling tool when presented with a novel cyclical event.

Chapter 8

Lesson 4: Constructing Chinese Characters (Chinese/History)

Enabling students to learn Chinese characters by turning the mechanical memorization of characters into meaningful memory and improving the efficiency of learning characters is a topic that has been explored and researched in teaching Chinese as a new language. This lesson uses the Inquiry Learning Model to guide students toward understanding Chinese characters as well as discovering patterns in the Chinese character system, with its complicated forms and various strokes.

After engaging in this lesson, students will find that the system of Chinese characters, despite its complexities, is a strong visual and regular character system. Through prompts and clues, teachers allow students to intuitively analyze and explore the composition of Chinese characters, gradually leading them to think in the direction of how Chinese characters are made and inspiring them to know and master more Chinese characters.

BACKGROUND INFORMATION FOR THE TEACHER

For beginners who are learning Chinese as a new language, the first thing they see is a set of symbols, but they don't know what these symbols represent. Introducing the methods of making Chinese characters can help students understand the structures of Chinese characters so that students can appreciate the relationship between the meanings and the compositions of Chinese characters while learning radicals and strokes.

They can also learn and comprehend Chinese culture by understanding Chinese characters because characters and culture are linked in Chinese more deeply than in most other languages. This lesson will pique the interest of students and broaden their horizons of learning the Chinese language and culture, thereby deepening their understanding of Chinese.

Chinese characters originated from pictures, using images as the carrier of interpretation. The formation of pictographs began with pictures depicting various aspects of nature; the picture forms gradually evolved into abstract symbols, and then through using image symbols as a form of written expression, they gradually developed and gained pronunciation. The method of making pictograph characters is the simplest and most basic method of making Chinese characters. An example of a pictograph character is 木 which represents a tree.

With the development of human society and the needs of life, people added abstract symbols mainly based on pictographs to indicate or refer to a thing, an object, or even an idea. These characters are called self-explanatory characters, which means that the meanings of these kinds of characters are self-presented or discernible from their appearances you observe. For example, "上" and "下" are two self-explanatory characters; "上" means "up" and "下" means "down." The meaning of the two characters are obviously discernible by simply looking at and comparing their structures. Pictographs and self-explanatory characters are the basic Chinese characters. They are composed of basic strokes, and each character is a whole that cannot be disassembled. For this reason, pictographs and self-explanatory characters are called single-type characters.

Later, people created associative compound characters by combining two or more single-type characters to form a new character to express a new meaning. An example of an associative compound character is 休, which represents resting. It is formed by combining the symbols for a person (on the left) and a tree (on the right). A person leaning against a tree is resting.

These three character-making methods are simple and important, but the number of Chinese characters formed by these three methods is quite small, and the range of application is limited, which does not fulfill the language's need for communication in daily life. Thus, people have developed pictophonetic characters based on pictographs, self-explanatory, and associative compound characters. A pictophonetic character is composed of two parts: a picto-symbol that represents meaning and a phonic-symbol that represents sound.

An example of a pictophonetic character is 洋, which represents the ocean. The left portion of the character represents water and gives the character meaning. The right portion of the character represents sheep, pronounced: "yang." This is the phonetic portion of the character, indicating that the character is pronounced; in this case, exactly like sheep.

This is a practical way to create new characters, so the pictogram characters have been greatly expanded since they came into being. Among modern Chinese characters, pictophonetic characters account for more than 90 percent of Chinese characters.

Lesson 4: Constructing Chinese Characters (Chinese/History) 79

As early as the Eastern Han Dynasty, Xu Shen, a scholar of the Eastern Han Dynasty, summarized six methods of making characters in the book *Shuo Wen Jie Zi (Analytical Dictionary of Characters)*, which is called "Liu Shu" (six categories or six scripts). Liu Shu is the earliest Chinese character system theory on the structure of Chinese characters, and it also provides the earliest analytical methods of Chinese characters that conform to its ideographic characteristics.

Nowadays, it is generally believed in the linguistic community that the pictographs, self-explanatory, associative compound, and pictophonetic in Liu Shu are word-making methods, while mutually explanatory and phonetic borrowing are methods of using words. Because the last two methods do not add new Chinese characters, they are not included in this lesson. The Inquiry Learning Model lesson on "The Methods of Making Chinese Characters" is suitable for those beginning to learn Chinese, who have mastered some basic strokes, radicals, and pinyin of Chinese characters.

Key Vocabulary and Terms

Analytical dictionary of characters
Associative compound characters
Evolution diagram
Mutually explanatory characters
Pictographic characters
Pictophonetic characters

Radicals
Self-explanatory characters
Six categories or six scripts
Stroke order
Strokes

Lesson Plan Objectives

Skills-Based Objectives

During this lesson, the students will:
- work cooperatively in small groups
- analyze primary and secondary source documents
- search for clues relative to the answers from various prompts
- obtain relative information from various schematic diagrams
- prepare questions based on the analysis of prompts and diagrams
- preliminarily form an integrated answer for the focus question
- develop the best conclusion for the focus question based on newly added information

Content-Based Objectives

During this lesson, the students will:
- Deduce and infer the methods of making Chinese characters based on Chinese character evolution diagrams and indicators in the lesson.

- Comprehend the meaning of new words created by adding indicators or putting together two or more pictographs based on the understanding of pictographs.
- Distinguish pictographs, self-explanatory associative compounds, and pictophonetic according to the methods of making characters.

Focus Question

Beginners in learning Chinese generally think that all Chinese characters are pictorial symbols. Considering the cognitive characteristics of beginners, how to design focus questions is particularly important for teachers. In long-term teaching practice of Chinese courses, our teachers found that the focus questions should not be too detailed.

First, too much information is difficult for students to digest and absorb; second, it narrows the imaginal space of students. Practical experience shows that it is more effective to stimulate students' curiosity by setting a brief and somewhat open-ended focus question.

Since the initial perception of students to Chinese characters is pictorial symbols, then a natural focus question is this: "Do you know how Chinese characters are made?" (Or, "Are all Chinese characters pictographs?") These questions may have multiple answers or may be hard to reach the final conclusion, but they will hook students into further exploration and thinking.

Procedures

See chapter 3 for detailed directions for implementing a lesson using the Inquiry Learning Model. Use this chapter as a reference as you set up this lesson. (Additionally, all of the graphics required to execute this lesson are available on the authors' website. See a link to the website in the introduction.)

Step 1: Investigate and Prepare

First, you need to be familiar with the background information about how Chinese characters are made in this lesson. Prepare yourself for the questions students may ask by familiarizing yourself with the prompts at the end of this chapter. Then, you may make a rough assessment of the language proficiency and personality traits of the students in the class and accordingly assign the roles for members of each group.

In order to promote good group dynamics, consider matching students with different learning levels and abilities into the same learning group and balance the groups. The specific grouping can be adjusted according to factors such as class size and personal qualities.

Lesson 4: Constructing Chinese Characters (Chinese/History) 81

At the beginning of the lesson, the teacher should present the procedure for this type of lesson, arrange the students in well-divided groups, and provide the lesson rules. Refer to the related content in the third chapter of this book (ideally, each group has three or four students), and provide a guide for each group, including rules, responsibilities, and role assignments. Let students sign their names after reading the guide and promise to abide by the relevant lesson rules.

Step 2: Introduce the Focus Question

Next, you introduce the focus questions. (See chapter 3, step 2 for details). Write down the focus question on the question board, such as, "Do you know how Chinese characters are made?" and then proceed to the questioning session.

Step 3: Question Session

This session is for students to analyze and discuss the content of each prompt. Prepare the object pictures related to the pictographs in prompt 1, including 口, 手, 水, 山, 人, 木, 雨, 鱼, 日, 月. The deliberate choice of these pictures also paves the way for the later prompts.

Prompt 1: Pictures Corresponding to the Pictographs

The first prompt of this lesson is a picture of real objects related to the pictographs. While the students are thinking about the correlation between the focus question and the pictures of the objects, let the students in each group discuss and say the name of each object (they can use their native language), to make sure that the students in each group know the objects depicted in the pictures. (This graphic is available on the authors' website. See the introduction for a link to that website.)

Give the students about five minutes to develop several yes/no questions about the prompt. They should consider how the prompt might relate to the focus question. Then take turns allowing each group to ask one question and answer it. The recorder in each group should be writing down the questions other groups ask as well as their answers to help them move closer to answering the focus question.

Prompt 2: Pictographic Characters

Next, pass out the second prompt and give the students a few minutes to develop several yes/no questions about it. It might help to remind them that they can look at the first prompt and perhaps will want to compare it with this prompt. The pictogram characters in this prompt will immediately attract students and stimulate them to be thinking deeply. During this time, the teacher should tour around the groups and listen carefully to the questions students are preparing.

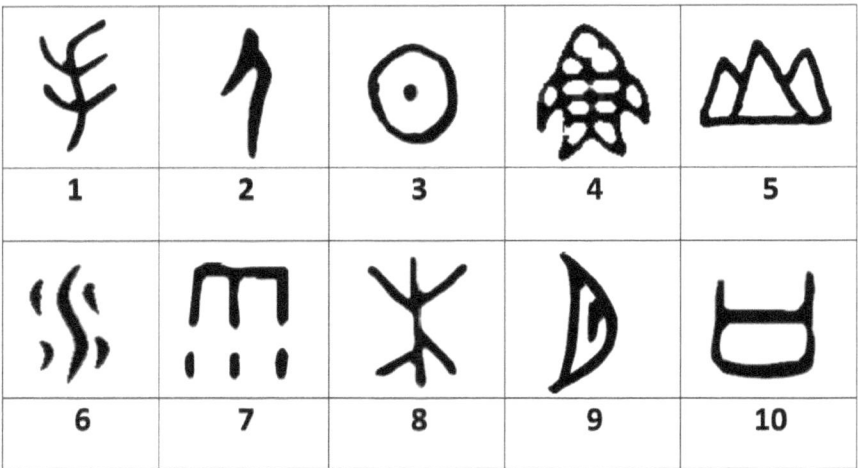

Source: Sherri Duan, used with permission

According to their experience, the teacher may arrange the order of questions from each group. This order should gradually increase students' understanding of the content and keep them thinking about the focus question. They may ask, "Are these characters close to the actual objects in the first prompt?" "We should find the real object that matches the corresponding character, shouldn't we?" When the group discussion is over, the students in each group are invited to ask questions in sequence according to the order decided previously. Be sure to only answer questions with a yes or a no.

You can refer to the related content in step 2 of chapter 3 for additional guidance about the procedure of this lesson. Give every group a chance to ask their question and ensure students are able to hear the questions and answers raised by each group. Teachers should encourage students to record the questions and answers as the information is cumulative and necessary for them to progress toward a solution to the focus question. (This image is available on the authors' website for download.)

Prompt 3: Pictogram Characters and Modern Chinese Characters

After confirming that the students understand the relationship and meaning of the real object pictures of prompt 1 and the characters of prompt 2, give picture prompt 3. After passing it out, tell them that this prompt is a type of matching exercise. There are modern Chinese characters and radicals on the right that correspond to the characters on the left. As mentioned earlier, if students first have learned the initial concepts of radicals and Chinese characters, it will be easier to inspire students to imagine associatively and find answers.

The completion of this step is used to assess whether students have a preliminary understanding of the focus question that how pictographs are produced. Let the students summarize how a real object image in prompt 1 is abstracted to a character in prompt 2, and then how it evolves to a modern Chinese character in prompt 3. This is the process by which pictographs are formed.

Pictograph characters developed gradually from visual outlines to abstract depictions to general symbols, in which the general image of a real object corresponds to the shape of the real object, with specific meaning and pronunciation. At this point in the lesson, the students probably know about the preliminary answer to the focus question. (As is the case with all of the graphics needed for this lesson, you may download the prompt 3 image from the authors' website. See the introduction for the link.)

Prompt 4: Associative Compounds

Now, the teacher gives prompt 4 and explains that this prompt is another matching exercise. Give the students a few minutes to try to complete the matching and then come up with several yes/no questions to ask. Through students' discussion and questioning and answering, students will generally understand that according to a certain relationship between objects, new Chinese characters can be produced and obtain meaning by combining corresponding characters. This kind of new character, composed of two or more single-type characters according to their relationship in meanings, is called an associative compound character.

We often see that in the class there is a decided advantage for those students who listen carefully to the questions the other groups pose. When students hear the answers the teacher provides and use the information from other groups' questions, they may change or refine their own questions. Teachers should encourage students to listen carefully to other groups, for it is a very effective classroom management strategy.

Once the first round is complete, including displaying prompts, group discussion, questioning by each group, and answering by the teacher, continue in this manner with the next prompt. As needed, the teacher may choose to rotate which group begins the questioning for each round, thus giving every group the same opportunity and encouraging more students to actively participate in the activities. (This graphic is available on the authors' website. Please refer to the introduction for the link.)

Prompt 5: Self-Explanatory Characters

Prompt 5 is another matching exercise. Students need to pay attention to the red arrows or marks on the pictures to notice that the character is referring to a specific part of the object. The picture of the knife indicates the blade. To create this character, the character for a knife (刀) is modified with a mark indicating which part of the knife the character represents, the sharp part of the 刀. What does it mean? Students may have many guesses, and the teacher should insist on answering yes or no. Ultimately, through the questions, students will find the connection between 刀 and 刃 and how one evolved into the other.

By analogy, since students already know that the pictograph 木 means a tree from prompt 1, what does it mean as a red mark pointing at the root of a tree? Xu Shen mentioned in the book *Shuo Wen Jie Zi*: "Self-explanatory characters mean knowing it as seeing it, understanding it by observing it, like 上 (up) and 下 (down). Characters of this type are called self-explanatory characters." (This graphic is available on the authors' website. Please refer to the introduction for the link.)

Step 4: Unveil Working Theories

At this point in the lesson, we suggest the teacher pause for a while and invite the groups to summarize the preliminary conclusions or answers to the focus questions. For example: from the prompts given, how many character creation methods have you inferred? What are their characteristics? Teachers may ask each group to write a sentence or a theoretical overview that summarizes their answers to the focus question. In the meantime, it is necessary for the teacher to walk around and observe among the study groups, occasionally help students to correct their words, question their assumptions or conclusions, or challenge the reliability of their evidence because the teacher's main responsibility is to guide students and not to tell them.

This process usually takes about 10 minutes, but the length of time may vary according to their ability levels. After the groups have completed their conclusions, you may invite one member of each group to come up to the board and write their group's theory; taking this opportunity, you may assess the entire class's understanding of the lesson content and any misconceptions that still persist. When students see the conclusions of other groups on the board, their thinking will be further expanded.

Moreover, this method is particularly useful for groups with obvious differences in the class. Once all groups have written down their preliminary conclusions on the board, you need to examine the accuracy of these conclusions. Remember not to overly criticize any conclusion, even if it is far from correct, for these conclusions, after all, are the best results of the students' hard work. If this lesson is taught using a virtual platform, students may post their theories using Jamboard or another similar whiteboard software so that all of the students may read through them. This type of platform also provides the teacher with the opportunity to comment on and even edit student theories. The point is to remind or highlight the conclusion closest to the final answer and encourage the students, referring to these conclusions, to do more in-depth thinking and explore the prompt content discussed.

Step 5: Continue to Display and Investigate the Remaining Prompts

Next, the teacher can continue to display the remaining prompts and allow teams to ask their yes/no questions. In the meantime, students should be allowed to modify their preliminary conclusions at any time in the succeeding links. Of course, the questioning can enable students to firmly grasp the prompt materials and conduct more thinking, discussion, and exploration around the focus questions, thereby deepening their understanding of character-making methods of pictographs, self-explanatory and associative compounds.

When the students are so excited about having found the answer to the focus question, tell them that these three types of characters are pure ideograph and, in essence, within the category of pictograph and only account for about 10 percent of modern Chinese characters. So, what are other methods of making Chinese characters?

Prompt 6: Phonic Symbols of Pictophonetic Characters

After students understand how the above ideographic characters are formed, give prompt 6 and ask students to analyze the features of the characters. The purpose is to let students find out the similarities and differences between these words. The students will soon discover what they have in common. With the word 青 on the right for each of them, all characters pronounce the sound "qing." We should tell the students that the radicals that relate to the

Source: Sherri Duan, used with permission

pronunciation of these characters are called phonetic radicals or phonic symbols. Ask the students to find out the radicals they have learned from prompt 6, such as 晴, 清, 蜻, 鲭, and so on. (This graphic is available for download on the authors' website.)

Prompt 7: Picto-Symbols of Pictophonetic Characters

The characters in prompt 6 have the same pronunciation but nothing in common in meaning. At this time, give the students a group of pictophonetic characters containing the radical character 虫 (worm) and let them discuss the characteristics of these characters in prompt 7. Linking with the images in prompt 7, the students may quickly understand the relationship between the meaning of the word *worm* and *ants, butterflies, dragonflies, earthworms, spiders*, and *tadpoles*.

Synthesizing the radicals connected with the meaning and the radicals connected with the sound of the characters in prompt 6, how should the character 蜻 in prompt 7 be pronounced? Students can be reminded that they still have all of the previously distributed prompts at their desks. The radicals found in prompt 3, 氵, 口, 扌, 鱼, 日, 木, 亻, 山, might be useful. So, what does the character on the left side of the character 蜻 mean?

In this character, the picto-symbol 虫 is on the left, and the phonic-symbol 青 (qing) is on the right. The combination of this left picto-symbol and this right phonetic-symbol refers to the pictophonetic character, which means dragonfly. Note that while this character 青 means "green" and that dragonflies may be green, the symbol in this character is there only for phonetic purposes and shows that the character is pronounced "qing." The dragonfly, with its left-picto, and right-phonetic orientation, is the most common, accounting for almost 80 percent of the modern pictophonetic characters.

Of course, in pictophonetic characters, there are also right picto-symbol with left phonic-symbol, up picto-symbol with down phonic-symbol, down picto-symbol with up phonic-symbol, outside picto-symbol with inside phonic-symbol, inside picto-symbol with outside phonic-symbol. All of these only accounts for about 20 percent of the pictophonetic characters. It should be noted that our primary purpose in this lesson is to let students deduce the rules of the methods of making Chinese characters through continuous exploration and thinking with the prompts given by the teacher, thus encouraging students to understand and master more Chinese characters after they, on learning by analogy, comprehend the methods of making Chinese characters. (This graphic is available for download on the authors' website. See the introduction for the link.)

Step 6: Revise and Improve the Theories and Discuss

With a deepening understanding of the course content and topics, you may ask students to reexamine their original conclusions and make amendments or improvements. Depending on the remaining time in the class period, you may invite representatives of the groups to state their answers to the focus questions and push students to discuss the connections between the prompts. In the meantime, encourage students to ask open questions about the lesson theme.

Teachers can use this opportunity to pass on missing information to students during the answering process. For example, due to the evolution of pronunciation, some pictophonetic characters can no longer be recognized as pictophonetic characters according to modern Chinese pronunciation. As an example, the character 骡 (mule) is no longer pronounced as the right-phonetic symbol suggests. There are also local dialects, like the way people from Boston have a unique manner of speaking American English. This adds another layer of complexity to the Chinese language.

Additionally, due to the evolution of Chinese character forms and other reasons, some picto-symbols can no longer correctly represent the meaning of the character. An example of this is the character 骄. You may notice the radical for the horse on the left (马); it is the same radical as the left portion of the character for the mule above. But this character represents pride; a relationship to horses is no longer apparent.

Step 7: Evaluate and Reflect

The last step of this lesson is to have the students reflect on their learning. This can be accomplished by having them write in the evaluation and feedback form found in chapter 4 of this book. In this lesson, the students explore different forms of Chinese characters rather than listen to the teacher's lecture on the subject. The inquiry process fully uses students' imagination, sharpens their observation skills, makes learning Chinese characters fun, and broadens their vision of learning Chinese, thereby improving their ability to understand and apply Chinese characters.

Prompt 8: Quiz

As a final exercise, you can give a quiz (below) as an exit ticket to assess their learning of these characters during the lesson. (This graphic is available for download on the authors' website. See the introduction for the link.)

Source: Sherri Duan, used with permission

Chapter 9

Lesson 5: Exploitation and Immortality

The Story of Henrietta Lacks (ELA/Biology/History)

BACKGROUND INFORMATION FOR THE TEACHER

This lesson will most commonly be part of a US history unit in the twentieth century with a focus on the civil rights movement and African American history. It may also be placed within the context of women's rights, women's reproductive rights, or medical ethics. A broader thematic connection could be made in science or history classrooms with medical ethics and the experiments conducted during World War II by Mengele and Ishii. Additional connections can be made in a humanities/ELA classroom in reading about disadvantaged communities and the role race played juxtaposed within mid-twentieth-century American society.

Henrietta Lacks was born Loretta Pleasant in 1920, to parents who were the children of slaves. When Lacks's mother died giving birth to her 10th child, her father, ill-equipped to raise 10 children on his own, distributed them to willing extended family members around the state of Virginia. Thus, at age four, Lacks started a new life on her paternal grandfather's tobacco farm. Among the other children living with her grandfather was David Lacks, Henrietta's older first cousin.

The circumstances surrounding Henrietta's early relationship with David are unclear. However, it is known that Lacks gave birth to her first child with David at the age of 14 and her second a few years later. She married David at age 20 and moved from Virginia to Maryland, where David took up work in the steel industry. Altogether Lacks had five children before the age of 30, her last, a son named Joseph, was born at the Johns Hopkins Medical Hospital in Baltimore, Maryland.

Johns Hopkins, within a half-hour of the Lacks' home, was the only hospital nearby that provided medical care to African Americans. Within months of Joseph's birth, Lacks was diagnosed with cervical cancer and began a short, unsuccessful treatment regimen at the hospital. At the time of diagnosis, a Johns Hopkins doctor removed samples of Lacks's tumor for analysis. The doctor passed these cells on to Dr. George Gey, a cancer researcher at Johns Hopkins. It is at this point in the story of Henrietta Lacks that the details shift toward a scientific focus.

SCIENTIFIC AND MATHEMATICAL CONNECTIONS

The Henrietta Lacks story is about vaccines, cancer, genetics, and medicine. In particular, the lesson is tied to biology in several strands that are commonly included in high school biology courses. The best and most common strand is genetics. A normal cell reproduces itself by a cell division process called mitosis. Mitosis is a process in which a cell divides into two identical cells that are also identical (genetically) to the original cell. The division proceeds through five phases. Most of the life of a cell is in the nondividing phase called interphase. The body will decide when a cell needs to divide—perhaps it is for repair of an injury or the cell is in the growth plate of a bone when a child is in a growth spurt.

There is a gene that turns on the division process and turns it off. When the gene signals the cell to initiate the divide sequence, the cell enters prophase. In this phase, the DNA in the nucleus will replicate itself so that there will be two sets of chromosomes—enough for two daughter cells. Then the other phases ensue: metaphase where the chromosomes line up along the equator of the cell in pairs; anaphase, where the chromosome pairs migrate apart toward opposite poles; and telophase where the cell splits in half. Then there are two identical cells that can then grow in interphase until they receive a signal to initiate the mitosis sequence again.

This is the life of a normal cell. The cancer cell divides in exactly the same way, but it does not turn off the divide sequence, so it divides continuously. A tumor is a mass of cells that have divided over and over again when the body does not need it. The cancer cells harvested from Henrietta Lacks's tumor are called HeLa cells. These HeLa cells have been continuously dividing since they were taken from Henrietta in 1951. Tons of cells have been produced. Doctors simply feed the cells and they divide continuously. These cells are even present today in nearly every biology lab in the country.

Before tackling a few more science connections, here is a mathematical connection. How many cells have the original cells that were taken from Henrietta divided into? The book, *The Immortal Life of Henrietta Lacks* by Rebecca Skloot (2011) contains an estimate that the mass of HeLa cells grown since 1951 is similar to the mass of a blue whale.

You could calculate an estimate of the maximum possible division rate and see how that compares to a whale. Since a conservative estimate of the life cycle of a cell is one hour—well-fed bacteria cells will go through a generation in less than half that time—one could calculate the possible number of generations since 1951. This was over 70 years ago.

In 70 years there are over a half-million hours—613,620 hours is 70 times 365.25 times 24. If you started with one cell, and, after an hour you had two cells and after another hour you had four cells, and so on, today the number of cells would be 2 raised to the 613,620 power. This is a number that normal computers cannot calculate. Many computers can only deal with a number that is 2 raised to the 1,023 power, a number that is over 300 digits long.

If these cells really did double in size every hour, today, they would more than fill the Milky Way galaxy. If you want to know how long, at this rate it would take to reach the mass of a blue whale, it is only about 52 hours, only four days after. The cells would reach the mass of the earth in only 119 hours. This is using the ballpark estimate of 50 million cells per gram. Clearly, the estimate of a blue whale is not an impossibility.

There is an interesting book about geometric progressions called *One Grain of Rice* by Demi (1997). The story is about a girl named Rani who tricks the greedy king into giving her his stockpile of rice. Rani is owed a favor by the king and simply asks for one grain of rice today, and two grains tomorrow and four grains the next day and so on for 30 days. This amounted to the king's entire store of rice, which Rani fed to the hungry people. While this book may target a younger audience, it is an engaging read and presents a sophisticated mathematical concept for secondary and early college students.

The story of Henrietta Lacks is also about vaccinations and the immune system. This is a topic that has a minor piece of most high school biology curricula. In the 1940s and early 1950s, polio was a much-feared disease. Polio is a virus. It is not treatable with antibiotics. Penicillin was first used in 1928 and dramatically reduced the incidence of bacterial infections. But a virus is not a bacterium. Unlike bacteria, a virus is not a cell. A virus is a package of DNA inside a protein shell. It does not have the necessary cell parts to survive on its own. As such, it needs to live inside of another cell. Inside, it replicates itself repeatedly, feeding off the host cell.

The human immune system fights viruses in a number of ways. One way is by producing antibodies. Antibodies are proteins that the body produces when it detects a foreign substance, such as a virus. The antibody attaches to the virus and "recruits" white blood cells to devour it. The antibody is specific to a given virus because at the molecular level, its effectiveness is dependent on the shape of the molecule. Therefore, an antibody for one virus can only attach to that specific virus.

The body produces antibodies as soon as it detects a virus. These antibodies will be present in your system indefinitely, so they will be present if this virus invades the body again. When the polio virus attacks the body, the problem is that the immune response is not fast enough and the virus multiplies to a large number before the antibodies can be produced. The immune system is behind the virus and is unable to catch up and eliminate the virus.

The development of a vaccine against polio is tied to Lacks and her cancer cells. Dr. Jonas Salk developed a vaccine in which he injected a killed polio virus into a subject. This killed virus is incapable of reproducing, so it cannot cause the disease, but its presence is enough to trigger the production of antibodies.

A vaccinated individual then has antibodies that can attack the real virus as soon as it invades the body, before it can take hold. That is how a vaccine works, but how is that connected to Henrietta Lacks? Before Salk's vaccine could be used, it needed to be tested to see if it provided immunity.

Testing involved inoculating a child and then mixing the child's blood serum (which hopefully would contain antibodies) with a live poliovirus and some cells. If the serum contained antibodies, the virus would not be able to infect the cells. The scientists would be able to tell this using a microscope. Prior to the discovery of HeLa cells, the source of cells had been monkeys. When a test was to be run, a monkey would be killed and its cells would be harvested for the test. The desire for human cells to run this test came not out of a concern for animals—in the 1950s there was not a public outcry for animal rights—the desire came from finances. It was really expensive to obtain cells from monkeys.

Salk's idea was to test two million samples. A field test of this magnitude had not been attempted due to the cost, estimated in millions of dollars. The HeLa cells were an inexpensive alternative and made this test financially viable. In the years since the polio vaccine, HeLa cells have played a vital role in the development of countless other medical advances.

Key Vocabulary and Terms

Antibodies
Cancer
Cell research
Civil rights
DNA

Jonas Salk
Mitosis
Polio
Proteins
Racism

Genetics
Immune system
Immunity

Tumor
Vaccine
Virus

Lesson Plan

Skills-Based Objectives
During this lesson the students will
- work cooperatively in small groups
- analyze primary and secondary source documents
- reconcile information from multiple maps
- develop questions based on document analysis
- advance a hypothesis that answers the focus question
- modify the hypothesis as information is added

Content-Based Objectives
During this lesson the students will
- analyze the impact of socioeconomic status on the life of Henrietta Lacks
- identify the way race limited Henrietta Lacks's options throughout her life
- consider the rationality of scientific use of an individual's cells

Focus Question

The focus question for this lesson is, "Whose cells are they?" Unlike some of the other lesson's focus questions, this question is a significant clue, indicating to the students that the topic has something to do with a person's cells. Because this lesson is rich with layers of learning embedded within the fields of civil rights, human rights, women's reproductive rights, African American history, and medical ethics, uncovering the central strand of the inquiry gives little away. If a more abstract question is required, one could ask, "What are the ethical issues surrounding this person's death?"

Procedures

Please refer to chapter 3 for detailed instructions regarding the setup and steps for an inquiry lesson. (All of the images necessary for this lesson are available on the authors' website. See the introduction for a link to that website.) Prior to the start of class, remember to arrange your prompts in a location that is easy for you to access, but also separate from your students. Select your groups (three or four students in a group ideally) and arrange desks to facilitate group interaction.

Write the focus question, "Whose cells are they?" in the location you have chosen that will allow you to disclose the question at the appropriate time.

Step 1: Investigate and Prepare

This step has been completed for you. Be familiar with the background information above so that you are knowledgeable and prepared to answer questions that the students will ask. (All of the prompts necessary to teach this lesson are available on the authors' website. Please see the introduction for a link to that website.)

Step 2: Introduce Focus Question

At the beginning of class, settle the students into their groups and explain the rules of the mystery game they are about to play (see chapter 2 for details). Provide each group with one copy of the rules at the outset. You might even want your students to sign that paper as a pledge that they will endeavor to follow the rules. Introduce the focus question for the day and proceed directly with the first prompt. (The graphic organizers necessary for this lesson are available on the authors' website.)

Step 3: Start Questioning Rounds

The next segment of class will be devoted to students' analysis of the various documents and prompts required for the lesson.

Prompt 1: Image of Henrietta Lacks

The first document suggested for this lesson is the photograph of Henrietta Lacks. There is little known about this photograph other than it must have been taken when Lacks was in her 20s, most likely in Maryland. The photograph purposely has Lacks's birth and death date under it. This information should move the students to think about why her life was so short. Combined with the focus question prompt, students should decipher that Lacks's cells are a key part of the lesson.

They may or may not also suppose that her race is an important element in the mystery to be solved. Give students a specific number of minutes to talk in their groups about the photograph. At the end of this specified time, usually roughly five minutes, the students must be ready with two or more questions to ask you. And remember, the questions must be asked in such a way as to be answerable with a yes or a no.

During the five minutes students are analyzing the clue, circulate among the groups and listen to the questions the students are developing. You might find that calling on groups in a particular order based upon their questions might be beneficial to the class' accumulated understanding of the puzzle they are trying to solve. You might also find that you need to direct or redirect groups at times. For instance, if during your circulation of the room you notice that a group is disregarding the dates under Lacks's photograph, you might want to subtly point their attention to this detail.

Source: Science Source

When the analysis time is up, invite the students to raise their hands to ask you their group's question. Be sure to insist that the question they ask is answerable with a yes or a no. (Review the steps to the model in chapter 2 for clarification.) Give each group the opportunity to ask their question, ensuring that the class can hear both the questions and the answers. Encourage the students to take notes on the facts that are being accumulated by the questions.

96   Chapter 9

You may choose to rotate which group begins the questioning for each round so the same group does not ask the first question in every round. As you will see, there is a decided advantage to those students who listen carefully to the questions posed by other groups. When students listen to the answer provided by the teacher and process the information provided by their classmates, they may change or hone their own questions. Encouraging students to listen carefully to the other groups also acts as an effective classroom management strategy.

Once the first prompt question round is complete, proceed in this manner with the next several artifacts.

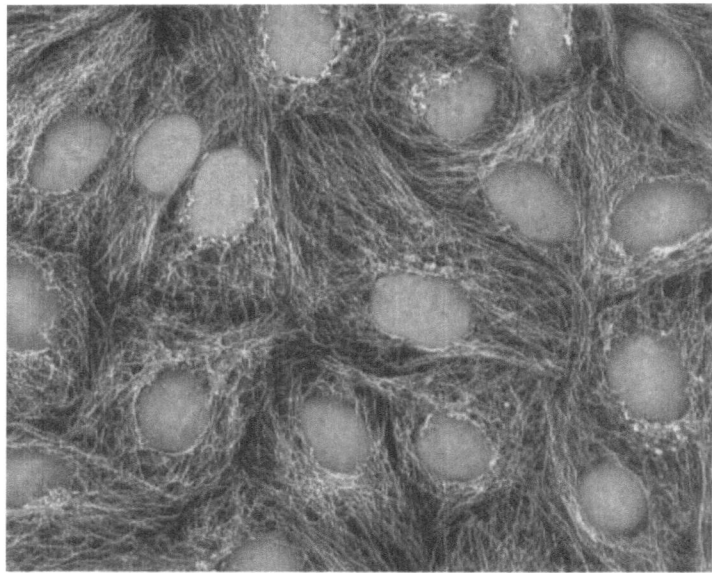

Source: https://commons.wikimedia.org/wiki/File:HeLa-I.jpg

Prompt 2: Photograph of HeLa Cells

This colorful clue will allow the students to connect Henrietta Lacks with the cells referenced in the focus question. With little information to go on at this stage in the lesson, students typically ask questions regarding illness and commonly learn that Lacks died from a form of cancer. At this point in the lesson, students are still missing the crucial characteristic of HeLa cells, which is their aggressive and astonishingly unique reproductive nature. (This image is available on the authors' website for download and use in this lesson. A link to the website may be found in the introduction.)

Prompt 3: Book Excerpt on Dr. George Gey and Photograph of Dr. Gey (Pronounced Guy)

This excerpt comes from the book, *The Immortal Life of Henrietta Lacks* by Rebecca Skloot (2011). This book, an excellent resource on this topic, explores the reasons why Gey so unabashedly accepted the cells from Lacks: Gey was single-minded in the pursuit of a line of perpetual cells that could be used in scientific research.

Gey and his lab were the first to note that Lacks's cancer cells were a perpetual line, one that would change the face of medical research forever. Indeed, his own words represent his relentless pursuit of a perpetual cell line when he characterizes himself as "the world's most famous vulture, feeding on human specimens almost constantly" (Skloot, 2011, p. 30).

David Lacks initially refused to grant permission for an autopsy. The doctors at Johns Hopkins suggested to him, however, that the information they gained from the autopsy might help his children in the future. After considering this, David Lacks granted permission for the autopsy. Permission thus given, the doctors were free to take tissue samples from Lacks that would be used in future research.

This prompt often draws students to the assumption that Gey was Lacks's doctor. In fact, he was not her doctor, and it is questionable whether Gey ever met Lacks. If he did, there were no witnesses to the meeting. Nonetheless, Gey plays a central role in the fate of Lacks's cells and their future use in medical research. (Both the book excerpt and photograph are available for download on the authors' website.)

Prompt 4: Lyrics to the Song, "Helen Lane"

This prompt reveals many of the details of Lacks's life that are not provided in the prompts preceding this round of inquiry. It is recommended that the students each be given a copy of the song lyrics. This differs from the recommendations for the other prompts—that each group only be given one copy of the prompt. Because this is such a long text document, it has been found that students are more able to interpret information if they are allowed time to read through and write on the document. Be prepared to copy a class set of the song lyrics.

The song is also very expressive; it is recommended that the students receive their copy of the song lyrics, be provided a few minutes to read it through, then listen to the song. After listening to the song, provide students with a few minutes to analyze and develop questions for this round of inquiry. The song, in addition to the prompts regarding Dr. Gey, allows students to question whether or not Lacks was treated fairly within the medical system of the 1950s. These prompts facilitate an opportunity for further discussion following the lesson. (Lyrics to the Helen Lane song are available on the authors' website. See the introduction for the link.)

Step 4: Unveil Working Theories

It is at this point that we recommend you pause and invite the students to write a preliminary theory in answer to the focus question, "Whose cells are they?" Ask each group to craft one sentence that sums up their response to the question. Circulate and assist students with wording, challenge their assumptions and ask for evidence as they work. This process typically takes about 10 minutes, but may vary depending on the skill level of the students and their experience with inquiry.

As groups finish composing sentences, invite one person from each group to write their response on the board. This process also allows the teacher to assess the entire class for misconceptions, misinterpretations, and general understanding. As students see other groups' hypotheses on the board, it may help advance their own thinking. This is especially helpful in classrooms that are heterogeneously grouped. If this lesson is taught using a virtual platform, students may post their theories using Jamboard or another similar whiteboard software so that all of the students may read through them. This type of platform also provides the teacher with the opportunity to comment on and even edit student theories.

Step 5: Investigate Remaining Prompts

Return to the questioning process, using the remaining prompts. This will allow students to continue to modify their theories.

Prompt 5: Chart, Reported Cases of Polio, 1940–2000

This prompt moves students to question what might be a burgeoning answer to the focus question, "Whose cells are they?" Students might have been tempted to answer this question with a simple response, "They are Henrietta Lacks's cells." In fact, because of the impact Lacks's cells have had on medical research, it could be argued that her tissue belongs to the ages, so to speak.

The question most often presented by students in this round of inquiry is, "Did Henrietta Lacks's cells have something to do with the cure for polio?" They are impelled to ask this question based on the dates for development of the polio vaccine and the year Lacks died. Once they determine that HeLa cells were crucial to the creation of the polio vaccine, the question regarding the legitimacy of medical science's claim on HeLa cells becomes much more blurred.

Once all the groups have written statements on the board, review them for accuracy. Be cautious not to overly criticize a theory that is far off the mark. The theory is, after all, the students' best working idea. Highlight the statements that come close to summing up the situation at play and encourage students to use those statements or segments of statements to continue their thinking. (This chart, and all of the resources for this lesson are available for download on the authors' website. See the introduction for a link to that website.)

Resume with the remaining inquiry and question rounds until all the prompts have been distributed.

Prompt 6: Historical Marker of Henrietta Lacks, Clover, Virginia

Source: Bernard Fisher, used with permission http://www.hmdb.org

Prompt 6 is a historical marker that fills in a few more details of Lacks's life, as well as reinforcing some details provided by the song lyrics. The sign questions the ethics of Lacks's cell use and indicates that her cells were used in multiple lines of research for the common good. This prompt also informs students that Lacks's cells were valued for their ability to reproduce, a unique and "extraordinary" characteristic.

Prompt 7: News Article, "Henrietta Lacks's Family, Feds Reach Settlement," by Malcolm Ritter, August, 2013

The final prompt, as is the case with almost all the final prompts presented in the book, fills in most of the remaining details the students still lack. This article briefly reviews the history of Lacks's life and brings the reader up to date on the treatment of her cells and the family's right to those cells. It doesn't clarify the more ethical question of "Whose cells are these?" However, it does at the very least explain that the family is being credited and in some ways compensated for Lacks's contribution to medical science. (This article is available for download on the authors' website. Please see the introduction for a link.)

Step 6: Revise Theories and Discuss

After a final round of questioning, move to the final step in the model. Ask students to revisit their written statement and make modifications based on their more developed understanding of the problem presented. Depending on time remaining, invite one to three groups to present their statements in answer to the focus question. Use their work as a jumping off point to discuss the mystery behind HeLa cells. It is at this point that you can invite the students to openly ask you questions about the topic and you can freely fill in the gaps in their understanding. Once questions have been answered and possible misconceptions clarified, ask students to use the Wrap-Up Graphic Organizer to reflect on their understanding of how the lesson went. The use of the reflective rubric referenced in the differentiation section of the lesson would be appropriate for all learners to complete and reflect upon.

Step 7: Evaluate and Reflect

The last step in this lesson is to evaluate student learning. The lesson is flexible in that the focus can be placed on many different topics in American history: civil rights, human rights, women's rights, and medical ethics. The evaluation should focus on the specific learning objectives you have targeted for your students.

Refer to the end of chapter 4 for specific examples of differentiated strategies for the Henrietta Lacks lesson.

Chapter 10

Lesson 6: China's Maritime Might (Economics/History)

Like many Inquiry Learning Model lessons in the humanities and social sciences, this inquiry question has many answers. The goal of this lesson is to provide students with evidence for some of the factors that contributed to China becoming an early leader in global maritime trade.

The lesson may be used as a Chinese history lesson focused on the Ming dynasty, its tribute system, and trade. While students may know the fundamentals of the story of Admiral Zheng He, they have likely not considered the combined economic, political, and technical factors as presented in this lesson.

BACKGROUND INFORMATION FOR THE TEACHER

This lesson may be used as an introduction to China's most recent leadership role in global trade. From the Silk Road to Zheng He's treasure voyages, China's current global trade leadership in the Asia Pacific is another chapter in a long history of open, extensive, and beneficial trade.

In President Xi Jingping's 2015 speech before the National Committee on US-China relations in Seattle, Washington, he indicated that "as far as the existing international system is concerned, China has been a participant, builder, and contributor." China is investing heavily in the Asia Pacific region as well as across the continent of Africa. As other world powers shift their focus inward, China is once again emerging as a global trading partner and leader in trade. Revisiting China's past successes in this area will build students' understanding of China's leadership on the world stage not as a recent phenomenon but as a historical mainstay.

At the start of the 15th century, naval admiral Zheng He was appointed by the Emperor Yongli of the Ming dynasty to conduct trade and gather tribute across the greater Asia Pacific region. Admiral Zheng conducted seven great voyages that took him from Nanjing to the city of Mombasa in present day Kenya and parts of present-day Indonesia. The treasure voyages, as they came to be called, were most famous for the impressively large fleet that far surpassed any naval fleet in existence at that time, and indeed for some time to come.

The fleet consisted of more than 300 ships with a crew of close to 30,000 men. Entire ships were dedicated to carrying food, livestock, and water to keep the fleet provisioned. Dozens more ships carried troops, diplomats, goods for trade, and tribute to return to the emperor.

Natives along the coast of east Africa were often quoted as describing the fleet's arrival as something otherworldly, terrifying, and incomprehensible in size. Fortunately for those natives, Admiral Zheng traveled not with the intent to conquer but with the intent to trade, establish partnerships, and demonstrate China's great political and technical strength.

The Ming treasure voyages were successful because of the confluence of political strength, maritime invention, and trade expertise. The lesson that follows highlights each of those categories through the use of maps, documents, and artifacts that students may explore as they work to answer this inquiry question: "How did China create the first maritime global trade network?"

The lesson begins with factors that contributed to China's naval superiority and the strength of Admiral Zheng's fleet: bamboo watertight ship construction, the compass, and intricate silk sails. From that foundation, the lesson shifts to an examination of trade routes, the relationship between Confucian values of leadership and the Ming's success, and evidence of the government's support of the expeditions and trade endeavors.

Finally, the lesson examines the benefits of trade for those who encountered the fleet and for China. Examples such as porcelain and a giraffe, delivered to the royal court, are highlighted. Finally, the lesson ends with a map of Admiral Zheng's seven voyages.

Key Vocabulary and Terms
Global trade   Tribute system
Maritime   Vessel
Treasure voyage

Lesson Plan Objectives
Skills-Based Objectives
During this lesson the students will:
- work cooperatively in small groups
- analyze primary and secondary source documents
- reconcile information from multiple maps

Lesson 6: China's Maritime Might

- develop questions based on document analysis
- advance a hypothesis that answers the focus question
- modify the hypothesis as information is added

Content-Based Objectives
During this lesson the students will:
- connect multiple factors contributing to China's success
- recognize the historic and modern role China plays in global trade
- summarize the events surrounding the treasure voyages

Focus Question

The focus question for this lesson is "How did China create the first maritime trade network?" Often the question you decide upon will be dependent on the thematic focus you select for the lesson. Because this lesson has the potential to move in several different directions, you may find that a different question will serve your established learning objectives more effectively.

Procedures

Please refer to chapter 3 for detailed instructions regarding the setup and steps for an Inquiry Learning Lesson. Prior to the start of class, remember to arrange your prompts in a location that is easy for you to access but also separate from your students. Select your groups (three or four students in a group ideally) and arrange desks to facilitate group interaction. Write the focus question, "How did China create the first maritime trade network?" on the board. (All of the prompts for this lesson are available on the authors' website. Please see the introduction for a link.)

Step 1: Investigate and Prepare

This step has been completed for you. Be familiar with the background information above so that you are knowledgeable and prepared to answer questions that the students will ask.

Step 2: Introduce Focus Question

At the beginning of class, settle the students into their groups and explain the guidelines (see chapter 2 for details). Provide each group with one copy of the guidelines at the outset. You may even want them to sign the pledge that they will endeavor to follow the guidelines. Introduce the focus question for the day and proceed directly to the first prompt. The student guidelines handout and student contract are available for download on the authors' website.

Step 3: Start Questioning Rounds

The next segment of class will be devoted to students' analysis of the various prompts required for the lesson. Give students a specific amount of time to talk in their groups about the prompt. During this time, usually about five minutes, the students must prepare two or more questions to ask you. Circulate among the groups and listen to the questions the students are developing. You might find that calling on groups in a particular order based on their questions is beneficial to the class's accumulated understanding of the mystery they are trying to solve.

When the analysis round time is up, invite the students to raise their hands to ask you their group's question. Be sure to insist that the question they ask is answerable with a yes or a no. Review the steps in part I, chapter 2 for clarification. Give each group the opportunity to ask its question, ensuring that the class can hear both the questions and the answers.

Encourage the students to take notes on the facts that are being accumulated by the questions. (A downloadable version of the note sheets are available on the authors' website.) As you will see, there is a decided advantage for those students who listen carefully to the questions posed by other groups. When students listen to the answers provided by the teacher and process the information generated by their classmates' questions, they may change or refine their own questions. Encouraging students to listen carefully to the other groups also acts as an effective classroom management strategy.

Once the first questioning round is complete, continue in this manner with the next several prompts. You may choose to rotate which group begins the questioning for each round so that the same group does not ask the first question in every round.

Prompt 1: Bamboo Reed and Cross Section of Bamboo

Prompt 1 includes two images of bamboo. Bamboo has some incredible properties. It is strong, light, flexible, self-sustaining, a source of building materials and as the cross section hints, able to float on water because of the separate chambers. This item will immediately engage students and promote divergent thinking as students strive to make a connection between the focus question and the bamboo. It is important that the image is of a cross section of bamboo so that the chambers inside the wood are visible. (An image of a cross section of bamboo is available on the authors' website. See the introduction for a link to that website.)

Toward the end of this activity students may recognize the similarity between the interior hull of the Ming ships and the cross section of the

Lesson 6: China's Maritime Might 105

Source: https://freerangestock.com/photographer/Tobias-Eichner/1927

bamboo. There are many metaphorical connections to bamboo that will become apparent later in the lesson.

Prompt 2: An Excerpt from Louise Levathes's When China Ruled the Sea

By the start of the Ming Dynasty, the Chinese had advanced naval technology farther than any other nation or region in the world. Well before the Ming dynasty the Chinese had constructed boats with double hulls divided into watertight compartments reflecting the natural design of the bamboo reed. This protected the ship from sinking if it was rammed in battle.

As explained in Levathes's work, the watertight compartment also made it possible to store fresh water for long ocean voyages. Another innovation was the invention of the sternpost rudder which was attached to a rear post outside of the ship. The rudder could be raised and lowered depending on the depth of the water. This allowed larger ships to navigate closer to the coastline or in rivers where water levels are lower. (The excerpt from Levathes's book is available for download on the authors' website.)

106   Chapter 10

Prompt 3: Image of a Floating Magnetic Iron Compass and Excerpt from The Voyage of the Tail Wind (Shunfeng Xiangsong)

Prompt 3 is an image of a magnetic iron needle floating on a small stone basin of water. Magnetic iron compasses using water helped to mitigate the rocking motion of the ship and allow the needle to point to magnetic north. This innovation was responsible for China's leap onto the world maritime stage, allowing Zheng He's fleet to achieve the reach it did as early as the 15th century.

Along with the image of the compass, students should receive an excerpt from *The Voyage of the Tail Wind*, or *Shunfeng Xiangsong*, written in the 16th century. This excerpt reads like a poem that sailors might write, describing the value of the compass and their hope that the compass will keep them safe and on the correct path.

Prompt 4: Map of the Ten Thousand Countries of Earth

The Map of the Ten Thousand Countries of Earth was a joint project between Matteo Ricci and Chinese scholars and artisans of the Imperial Court. Matteo Ricci was a 16th-century Italian explorer and Jesuit priest. He lived in China for decades, where he earned a post within the royal court of the Chinese government and represented the Jesuit mission. The map he co-created places China at the center, suggesting its primary place in the world. The symbol for China translates to "middle kingdom" and 16th-century Chinese typically referred to land outside of the middle kingdom as barbarian lands. As a prompt, this map reveals the extent of maritime knowledge the Chinese had, as well as their world view. (An image of this map is available on the authors' website for download. Please refer to the introduction for the website address.)

Source: Library of Congress. Geography and Map Division. 1602 Kun Yu Wan Guo Quan Tu. Retrieved from the Library of Congress, https://www.loc.gov/item/2010585650

Step 4: Unveil Working Theories

At a point in the questioning rounds when you sense your students are homing in on a possible answer to the focus question, pause. With this lesson field tests indicated that this pause was usually most effective after prompt 4. Ask each group to craft one sentence, or a theory statement, that sums up their response to the focus question. As you circulate around the room, assist students with wording, challenge their assumptions, and ask for evidence as they work on this task. This process typically takes about 10 minutes, but the amount of time may vary depending on the skill level of the students.

As groups finish composing their sentences, invite one person from each group to write their response on the board. You can take this opportunity to assess the entire class for misconceptions, misinterpretations, and general understanding. As students see other groups' theories on the board, it may help advance their own thinking. This is especially helpful in classrooms that are heterogeneously grouped. (A graphic organizer is provided on the authors' website that you may use to assist students in the crafting of their theory statement. See introduction for the website address.) If this lesson is taught using a virtual platform, students may post their theories using Jamboard or another similar whiteboard software so that all of the students may read through them. This type of platform also provides the teacher with the opportunity to comment on and even edit student theories.

Once all the groups have written theories on the board, review them for accuracy. Be cautious not to overly criticize a theory that is far off the mark. The theory is, after all, the students' best working idea at the time. Highlight the theories that come close to summing up the situation under study, and encourage students to use those theories in their thinking.

Step 5: Investigate Remaining Prompts

Resume with the remaining prompts and questioning rounds until all the prompts have been distributed.

Prompt 5: Woodcut of Longjiang Shipyard and Levathes Excerpt

The Longjiang shipyard woodcut reveals the various workshops located in the Longjiang shipyard as well as bays where ships the size of the Ming fleet would have been constructed. The map reveals workshops for carpenters, sail makers, and ironsmiths on the left, with dry docks in the center which lead to the Yangtze River. Ships are illustrated in the woodcut, revealing the approximate number of ships that could be built simultaneously. This woodcut reinforces the strength and level of organization of China's maritime capabilities during the Ming dynasty. (The image of the shipyard woodcut is available on the authors' webpage. See the introduction for the website address.) Accompanying the image is an excerpt from Louise Levathes's *When China Sailed the Sea*. The excerpt includes information regarding when ships were ordered built, how many, and for what purpose.

Prompt 6: Painting of a Giraffe and a Ming Vase

The treasure fleet was created to replenish the imperial treasury after years of civil war. By reestablishing trade across the China Sea and the Indian Ocean, the Chinese would share in the lucrative profits of the spice trade up until this point enjoyed by pirates and bandits. The treasure fleet carried trade goods such as bolts of silk, cotton cloth, iron, salt, hemp, tea, wine, oil, and candles. In addition, vases and dishes made of porcelain from various regions of China were provided as trade items.

As illustrated in the book excerpt and image in prompt 5, the immense size of the armada was needed to haul the trade goods and supplies to far distances as well as to protect the vast wealth it carried. Once the treasure fleet set sail and China demonstrated its dominance, piracy lessened and the sea routes and trade was protected.

Source: https://picryl.com/media/tribute-giraffe-with-attendant-9083c7

In addition to practical goods that were traded, countries and regions paid tribute to the Ming dynasty through gifts unique to their region. One such example is the giraffe, illustrated in prompt six. This image depicts a giraffe being presented to the Ming court by the king of Bengal. Other animals, plants, and unique crafts were presented to Zheng He as tribute to the Ming. Likewise, the Chinese would trade their sought-after art with other regions. Accompanying the image of the giraffe is an image of a Ming vase typical of the type that would have been traded by the Ming fleet. (Both the image of the giraffe and the Ming vase are available on the authors' website for download and use. See the introduction for the website address.)

Step 6: Revise Theories and Discuss

Ask students to revisit their theory statement and make modifications based on their more developed understanding of the problem presented. Depending on time remaining, invite one to three groups to present their statements in answer to the focus question. Use their work as a jumping-off point to discuss China's domination of maritime global trade networks during the 15th century. It is at this point when you can invite the students to openly ask you questions about the topic and you can freely fill in the gaps in their understanding.

Step 7: Evaluate and Reflect

The last step in this lesson is to ask students to evaluate and reflect on their learning. This can be done using the Evaluation and Reflection Worksheet referenced chapter 4. (A sample Evaluation and Reflection Worksheet is shared in the authors' webpage. See the introduction for a link to that webpage.) China's domination of the global maritime trade lesson is flexible in that various themes in the social studies may be addressed—geography, technological innovations, imperial governance, and Ming history. The evaluation should focus on the specific learning objectives targeted for the students.

Note, when you reproduce these resources for your ILM lesson, be careful not to copy the caption. Providing students with the captions will give them more information than is necessary in the lesson.

References

Alshraideh, M. (2009). The effect of Suchman's inquiry model on developing critical thinking skills among university students. *International Journal of Applied Education Studies*, *4*(1), 58–69.

Aydeniz, M., Cihak, D. F., Graham, S. C., & Retinger, L. (2012). Using inquiry-based instruction for teaching science to students with learning disabilities. *International Journal of Special Education*, *27*(2), 189–206.

Bergman, D. (2011). Synergistic strategies: Science for ELLs is science for all. *Science Scope*, November, 40–44.

Black, E. (2012). *IBM and the Holocaust: The strategic alliance between Nazi Germany and America's most powerful corporation*. Dialog Press.

Bloom, B. (1993). *Bloom's taxonomy*. Addison-Wesley Longman Ltd.

Bloom, B. S. (Ed.). (1983). *Taxonomy of educational objectives: Book 1 cognitive domain*. Longman, Inc.

Boyle, E. D. (2000). *The Aral Sea: A lesson in environmental degradation*. National Library of Education.

Buehl, D. (2014). *Classroom strategies for interactive learning* (4th ed.). International Reading Association.

Cervone, B., & Cushman, K. (2012). *Teachers at work, six exemplars of everyday practice*. Jobs for the Future and the Nellie Mae Education Foundation.

Courtade, G. R., Browder, D. M., Spooner, F., & Dibiase, W. (2010). Training teachers to use an inquiry-based task analysis to teach science to students with moderate and severe disabilities. *Education and Training in Autism and Developmental Disabilities*, *45*(3), 378–399.

Crawford, T. (2003). From magic show to meaningful science. *Science Scope*, *27*(1), 36–39.

Demi. (1997). *One grain of rice*. Scholastic Press.

Dence, R., Cann, A., & Mobbs, R. (2006). Proceedings from the Association for Learning Technology, Annual Conference. University of Leicester. Piloting innovative uses of informal repositories in campus-based student assessment and associate tutor communities of practice.

Ellis, W. S., & Turnley, D. C. (1990). The Aral: A Soviet sea lies dying. *National Geographic*, *177*(2), 73–93.

Ferguson, R. (2003). *The devil and the disappearing sea: Or, how I tried to stop the world's worst ecological catastrophe*. Raincoast Books.

Feynman, R. (1999). *The pleasure of finding things out*. Basic Books.

Fradd, S. H., Lee, O., & Sutman, F. X. (2001). Promoting science literacy with English language learners through instructional materials development: A case study. *Bilingual Research Journal, 25*(4), 479–501.

Goodman, L., & Bernston, G. (2000). The art of asking questions: Using directed inquiry in the classroom. *The American Biology Teacher, 62*(7), 473–476.

Gregory, G., & Chapman, C. (2002). *Differentiated instructional strategies: One size doesn't fit all*. Corwin Press.

Grosslight, L. (1991). Understanding models and their use in science: Conceptions of middle and high school students and experts. *Journal of Research in Science Teacher, 28*, 799–822.

Gunter, M. A., Estes, T. H., & Schwab, J. (2003). *Instruction: A models approach*. A and B Publishing.

Hansen, L. (2006). Strategies for ELL success. *Science and Children*, January, 22–25.

Hempologydotorg. (2012, July 10). Ogunquit time lapse tide—12 hours in 34 seconds YouTube. Retrieved from https://www.youtube.com/watch?v=1DElJu5-g-I

Herczog, M. (2013). Q and A about the college, career, and civic life (C3) framework for social studies state standards. *Social Education, 77*(4), 218–219.

Housen, A., & Yenawine, P. (1999). *VTS visual thinking strategies: Understanding the basics*.

Ivany, G. (1969). The assessment of verbal inquiry in junior high school science. *Science Education, 53*(4), 287–293.

Jazzar, M. (2004). A new look at an old practice. *Principal Leadership, 5*(2), 34–39.

Jimenez, B. A., Browder, D. M., Spooner, F., & Dibiase, W. (2012). Inclusive inquiry science using peer-mediated embedded instruction for students with moderate intellectual disability. *Exceptional Children, 78*(3), 301–317.

Johnson, D. W., Johnson, R. T., & Holubec, E. J. (1990). *Cooperative learning in the classroom*. Association for Supervision and Curriculum Development.

Johnson, D. W., & Johnson, R. T. (1999). Making cooperative learning work. *Theory Into Practice, 38*(2), 67–73.

Jones, L. (1999). Shrinking of Aral Sea causes regional health crisis. *Washington Report on Middle East Affairs*, September 1999, 28–29.

Joyce, B., Weil, M., & Calhoun, E. (2004). *Models of teaching*. Pearson.

Kagan, S., & Kagan, M. (2009). *Kagan Cooperative Learning*. Kagan Cooperative Learning.

Lambroschini, A. (2008). *Aral Sea revived by dam*. Discovery Communications, LLC. http://dsc.discovery.com/news/2008/06/24/aral-sea.html

Levathes, L. (1997). *When China ruled the seas: The treasure fleet of the dragon throne*. Oxford University Press.

Lewis, S., Lee, O., & Santau, A. (2010). Student initiatives in urban elementary science classrooms. *School Science and Mathematics, 110*(3), 160–172.

Maor, E., & Barnard, R. W. (2016). *Trigonometry*. Encyclopedia Britannica, Inc.

Miller, A. (2015). *The crucible: A play in four acts*. Penguin Books.

Miller, B. (2012). Ensuring meaningful access to the science curriculum for students with significant cognitive disabilities. *Teaching Exceptional Children, 44*(6), 16–25.

Miller, K. (1999). *The peppered moth, an update.* http://www.millerandlevine.com/km/evol/Moths/moths.html

Minner, D. D., Levy, A. J., & Century, J. (2010). Inquiry-based science instruction—what is it and does it matter? Results from a research synthesis years 1984 to 2002. *Journal of Research in Science Teaching: The Official Journal of the National Association for Research in Science Teaching, 47*(4), 474–496.

Mobbs, M., Salmon, G., & Edirisingha, P. (2008). How to create podcasts—a practitioner's guide. In G. Salmon & P. Edirisingha (Eds.), *Podcasting for learning in universities* (pp. 188–204). McGraw-Hill and Open University Press.

National Council for the Social Studies (NCSS). (2013). *The College, Career, and Civic Life (C3) Framework for Social Studies State Standards: Guidance for enhancing the rigor of K–12 civics, economics geography, and history*. NCSS. p. 17.

National Governors Association Center for Best Practices, Council of Chief State School Officers. (2010). *Common Core State Standards*. National Governors Association Center for Best Practices, Council of Chief State School Officers, Washington, DC, http://www.corestandards.org/ELA-Literacy/RH/introduction.

Obama, B. H. (2013, August). *Remarks by the president on college affordability*, Buffalo, NY. http://www.whitehouse.gov/the-press-office/2013/08/22/remarks-president-college-affordability-buffalo-ny

Pray, L., & Monhardt, R. (2009). Sheltered instruction techniques for ELLs: Ways to adapt science inquiry lessons to meet the academic needs of English language learners. *Science and Children*, March, 34–38.

Ricketts, A. (2011). Using inquiry to break the language barrier: English language learners and science fairs. *The Science Teacher*, November, 56–58.

Ripple, R., & Bookcastle, V. (Eds.). (1964). *Piaget reconsidered*. Cornell University Press.

Ruebush, L. E., Grossman, E. L., Miller, S. A., North, S. W., Schielack, J. F., & Simanek, E. E. (2009). Scientists' perspective on introducing authentic inquiry to high school teachers during an intensive three-week professional development experience. *School Science and Mathematics, 109*(3), 162–174.

Schrenker, G. (1976). *The effects of an inquiry development program on elementary school children's science learning*. PhD thesis. New York University.

Schwab, J., & Brandwein, P. (Eds.). (1962). *The teaching of science: The teaching of science as enquiry and science in the elementary school*. Harvard University Press.

Shen, Xu. (2013). *Analytical dictionary of Chinese characters (说文解字)*. Zhonghua Book Company.

Silva, C., Weinburgh, M., Malloy, R., Smith, K. H., & Marshall, J. N. (2012). Towards integration. *Childhood Education, 88*(2), 91–95.

Skloot, R. (2011). *The immortal life of Henrietta Lacks*. Random House.

Suchman, R. J. (1962). *The elementary school training programme in science inquiry.* Report to the U.S. Office of Education, Project Title VII. University of Illinois Press.

Suchman, R. J. (1964). Illinois studies in inquiry training. *Journal of Research in Science Teaching, 2*(3), 230–232.

Tomlinson, C. A. (2017). *How to differentiate instruction in academically diverse classrooms* (3rd ed.). ASCD.

Watt, S. J., Therrien, W. J., Kaldenberg, E., & Taylor, J. (2013). Promoting inclusive practices in inquiry-based science classrooms. *Teaching Exceptional Children, 45*(4), 40–48.

The Weather Channel. (2022, September 6). *Monthly weather—Beijing.* The Weather Channel. https://weather.com/en-MT/weather/monthly/l/CHXX0008:1:CH

Willingham, D. (2010). *Why don't students like school: A cognitive scientist answers questions about how the mind works and what it means for the classroom.* Jossey-Bass.

Winchester, Simon (2002). *The map that changed the world.* Harper Perennial.

Yenawine, Philip. (1999). *Theory into practice: The visual thinking strategies* (pp. 1–11). Calouste Gulbenkian Foundation, Service of Education. https://vtshome.org/wp-content/uploads/2016/08/9Theory-into-Practice.pdf

About the Authors

Catherine Snyder is a National Board Certified Teacher and associate professor of education at Clarkson University. Her research in the field of inquiry learning encompasses her work with teacher education graduate students and has been the focus of several publications and presentations around the globe.

Mary Eads is a National Board Certified Teacher who has been teaching social studies for 33 years, and is an adjunct professor at Clarkson University.

Sean O'Connell is a National Board Certified Teacher who has been teaching for over 30 years as both a special educator and social studies classroom teacher. He received the *Murray Excellence in Teaching* award at Niskayuna High School and an *Excellence in Teaching* award from the State University of New York at Albany.

Richard Lasselle is a National Board Certified Teacher who has been teaching 36 years. He taught science at the middle school level, physics, chemistry, and Earth science. He is an assistant professor of STEM Education at Clarkson University.

Sherri Duan is an assistant professor of education at Clarkson University where she teaches Chinese grammar, linguistics, curriculum, and methods. In 2020, she received the *Outstanding Teaching* award from Clarkson University's Student Association and her book, *Research on "Jiang" Constructions from pre-Qin to Sui-Tang Dynasties*, was published in 2019.

Daniel Mattoon has been teaching mathematics and computer science for the past 19 years. He is a National Board Certified Teacher, a New York State Master Teacher, and won the *Presidential Award of Excellence for Mathematics Teaching* from President Obama in 2015.

Patricia Rand is a National Board Certified Teacher who taught high school English for 15 years before becoming an assistant professor of education at Clarkson University.

www.ingramcontent.com/pod-product-compliance
Lightning Source LLC
Chambersburg PA
CBHW021859230426
43671CB00006B/455